BioCritiques

Maya Angelou
Jane Austen
The Brontë Sisters
Lord Byron
Geoffrey Chaucer
Anton Chekhov
Stephen Crane
Emily Dickinson
William Faulkner
F. Scott Fitzgerald
Robert Frost
Ernest Hemingway
Langston Hughes
Stephen King
Arthur Miller
Toni Morrison
Edgar Allan Poe
J. D. Salinger
William Shakespeare
John Steinbeck
Mark Twain
Alice Walker
Walt Whitman
Tennessee Williams

Bloom's BioCritiques

TONI MORRISON

Edited and with an introduction by
Harold Bloom
Sterling Professor of the Humanities
Yale University

CHELSEA HOUSE PUBLISHERS
Philadelphia

SIDNEY B. COULTER LIBRARY
Onondaga Community College
4941 Onondaga Rd.
Syracuse, NY 13215

©2002 by Chelsea House Publishers,
a subsidiary of Haights Cross Communications.

Introduction © 2002 by Harold Bloom.

All rights reserved. No part of this publication may be reproduced or transmitted in any form or by any means without the written permission of the publisher.

Printed and bound in the United States of America

10 9 8 7 6 5 4 3 2

Library of Congress Cataloging-in-Publication Data
Applied for

ISBN 0-7910-6180-9

Chelsea House Publishers
1974 Sproul Road, Suite 400
Broomall, PA 19008-0914

http://www.chelseahouse.com

Contributing editor: Thomas March

Layout by EJB Publishing Services

Contents

User's Guide   vii

The Work in the Writer   ix
Harold Bloom

Introduction   1
Harold Bloom

Biography of Toni Morrison   3
Ellyn Sanna

Filling the Gaps: The Fictional World of Toni Morrision   39
Thomas March

Mixed Genres and the Logic
of Slavery in Toni Morrison's *Beloved*   61
Carl D. Malmgren

Community and Nature: The Novels of Toni Morrison   75
Barbara Christian

Chronology   93

Works by Toni Morrison   95

Works about Toni Morrison   97

Contributors   101

Index   103

User's Guide

These volumes are designed to introduce the reader to the life and work of the world's literary masters. Each volume begins with Harold Bloom's essay "The Work in the Writer" and a volume-specific introduction also written by Professor Bloom. Following these unique introductions is an engaging biography that discusses the major life events and important literary accomplishments of the author under consideration.

Furthermore, each volume includes an original critique that not only traces the themes, symbols, and ideas apparent in the author's works, but strives to put those works into cultural and historical perspectives. In addition to the original critique is a brief selection of significant critical essays previously published on the author and his or her works followed by a concise and informative chronology of the writer's life. Finally, each volume concludes with a bibliography of the writer's works, a list of additional readings, and an index of important themes and ideas.

HAROLD BLOOM

The Work in the Writer

Literary biography found its masterpiece in James Boswell's *Life of Samuel Johnson*. Boswell, when he treated Johnson's writings, implicitly commented upon Johnson as found in his work, even as in the great critic's life. Modern instances of literary biography, such as Richard Ellmann's lives of W. B. Yeats, James Joyce, and Oscar Wilde, essentially follow in Boswell's pattern.

That the writer somehow is in the work, we need not doubt, though with William Shakespeare, writer-of-writers, we almost always need to rely upon pure surmise. The exquisite rancidities of the Problem Plays or Dark Comedies seem to express an extraordinary estrangement of Shakespeare from himself. When we read or attend *Troilus and Cressida* and *Measure for Measure*, we may be startled by particular speeches of Ulysses in the first play, or of Vincentio in the second. These speeches, of Ulysses upon hierarchy or upon time, or of Duke Vincentio upon death, are too strong either for their contexts or for the characters of their speakers. The same phenomenon occurs with Parolles, the military impostor of *All's Well That Ends Well*. Utterly disgraced, he nevertheless affirms: "Simply the thing I am/Shall make me live."

In Shakespeare, more even than in his peers, Dante and Cervantes, meaning always starts itself again through excess or overflow. The strongest of Shakespeare's creatures—Falstaff, Hamlet, Iago, Lear, Cleopatra—have an exuberance that is fiercer than their plays can contain. If Ben Jonson was at all correct in his complaint that "Shakespeare wanted art," it could have been only in a sense that he may not have intended. Where do the personalities of Falstaff or Hamlet touch a limit? What was it in Shakespeare that made the two parts of *Henry IV* and *Hamlet* into "plays unlimited"? Neither Falstaff nor Hamlet will be stopped: their wit, their beautiful, laughing speech, their intensity of being—all these are virtually infinite.

In what ways do Falstaff and Hamlet manifest the writer in the work? Evidently, we can never know, or know enough to answer with any authority. But what would happen if we reversed the question, and asked: How did the work form the writer, Shakespeare?

Of Shakespeare's inwardness, his biography tells us nothing. And yet, to an astonishing extent, Shakespeare created our inwardness. At the least, we can speculate that Shakespeare so lived his life as to conceal the depths of his nature, particularly as he rather prematurely aged. We do not have Shakespeare on Shakespeare, as any good reader of the Sonnets comes to realize: they do not constitute a key that unlocks his heart. No sequence of sonnets could be less confessional or more powerfully detached from the poet's self.

The German poet and universal genius, Goethe, affords a superb contrast to Shakespeare. Of Goethe's life, we know more than everything; I wonder sometimes if we know as much about Napoleon or Freud or any other human being who ever has lived, as we know about Goethe. Everywhere, we can find Goethe in his work, so much so that Goethe seems to crowd the writing out, just as Byron and Oscar Wilde seem to usurp their own literary accomplishments. Goethe, cunning beyond measure, nevertheless invested a rival exuberance in his greatest works that could match his personal charisma. The sublime outrageousness of the Second Part of *Faust*, or of the greater lyric and meditative poems, form a Counter-Sublime to Goethe's own daemonic intensity.

Goethe was fascinated by the daemonic in himself; we can doubt that Shakespeare had any such interests. Evidently, Shakespeare abandoned his acting career just before he composed *Measure for Measure* and *Othello*. I surmise that the egregious interventions by Vincentio and Iago displace the actor's energies into a new kind of mischief-making, a fresh opening to a subtler playwriting-within-the-play.

But what had opened Shakespeare to this new awareness? The answer is the work in the writer, *Hamlet* in Shakespeare. One can go further: it was not so much the play, *Hamlet*, as the character Hamlet, who changed Shakespeare's art forever.

Hamlet's personality is so large and varied that it rivals Goethe's own. Ironically Goethe's Faust, his Hamlet, has no personality at all, and is as colorless as Shakespeare himself seems to have chosen to be. Yet nothing could be more colorful than the Second Part of *Faust*, which is peopled by an astonishing array of monsters, grotesque devils, and classical ghosts.

A contrast between Shakespeare and Goethe demonstrates that in each—but in very different ways—we can better find the work in the person, than we can discover that banal entity, the person in the work. Goethe to many of his contemporaries, seemed to be a mortal god. Shakespeare, so far as we know, seemed an affable, rather ordinary fellow, who aged early and became somewhat withdrawn. Yet Faust, though Mephistopheles battles for his soul, is hardly worth the trouble unless you take him as an idea and not as a person. Hamlet is nearly every-idea-in-one, but he is precisely a personality and a person.

Would Hamlet be so astonishingly persuasive if his father's ghost did not haunt him? Falstaff is more alive than Prince Hal, who says that the devil haunts him in the shape of an old fat man. Three years before composing the final *Hamlet*, Shakespeare invented Falstaff, who then never ceased to haunt his creator. Falstaff and Hamlet may be said to best represent the work in the writer, because their influence upon Shakespeare was prodigious. W.H. Auden accurately observed that Falstaff possesses infinite energy: never tired, never bored, and absolutely both witty and happy until Hal's rejection destroys him. Hamlet too has infinite energy, but in him it is more curse than blessing.

Falstaff and Hamlet can be said to occupy the roles in Shakespeare's invented world that Sancho Panza and Don Quixote possess in Cervantes's. Shakespeare's plays from 1610 on (starting with *Twelfth Night*) are thus analogous to the Second Part of Cervantes's epic novel. Sancho and the Don overtly jostle Cervantes for authorship in the Second Part, even as Cervantes battles against the impostor who has pirated a continuation of his work. As a dramatist, Shakespeare manifests the work in the writer more indirectly. Falstaff's prose genius is revived in the scapegoating of Malvolio by Maria and Sir Toby Belch, while Falstaff's darker insights are developed by Feste's melancholic wit. Hamlet's intellectual resourcefulness, already deadly, becomes poisonous in Iago and in Edmund. Yet we have not crossed into the deeper abysses of the work in the writer in later Shakespeare.

No fictive character, before or since, is Falstaff's equal in self-trust. Sir John, whose delight in himself is contagious, has total confidence both in his self-awareness and in the resources of his language. Hamlet, whose self is as strong, and whose language is as copious, nevertheless distrusts both the self and language. Later Shakespeare is, as it were, much under the influence both of Falstaff and of Hamlet, but they tug him in opposite directions. Shakespeare's own copiousness of language is well-nigh incredible: a vocabulary in excess of twenty-one thousand words, almost eighteen hundred of which he coined himself. And of his word-hoard, nearly half are used only once each, as though the perfect setting for each had been found, and need not be repeated. Love for language and faith in language are Falstaffian attributes. Hamlet will darken both that love and that faith in Shakespeare, and perhaps the Sonnets can best be read as Falstaff and Hamlet counterpointing against one another.

Can we surmise how aware Shakespeare was of Falstaff and Hamlet, once they had played themselves into existence? *Henry IV, Part I* appeared in six quarto editions during Shakespeare's lifetime; *Hamlet* possibly had four. Falstaff and Hamlet were played again and again at the Globe, but Shakespeare knew also that they were being read, and he must have had contact with some of those readers. What would it have been like to discuss Falstaff or Hamlet with one of their early readers (presumably also part of their audience at the Globe), if you were the creator of such demiurges? The question would seem nonsensical to most Shakespeare scholars, but then these days they tend to be either ideologues or moldy figs. How can we recover the uncanniness of Falstaff and of Hamlet, when they now have become so familiar?

A writer's influence upon himself is an unexplored problem in criticism, but such an influence is never free from anxieties. The biocritical problem (which this series attempts to explore) can be divided into two areas, difficult to disengage fully. Accomplished works affect the author's life, and also affect her subsequent writings. It is simpler for me to surmise the effect of *Mrs. Dalloway* and *To the Lighthouse* upon Woolf's late *Between the Acts*, than it is to relate Clarissa Dalloway's suicide and Lily Briscoe's capable endurance in art to the tragic death and complex life of Virginia Woolf.

There are writers whose lives were so vivid that they seem sometimes to obscure the literary achievement: Byron, Wilde, Malraux, Hemingway. But most major Western writers do not live that exuberantly, and the greatest of all, Shakespeare, sometimes appears to have adopted the personal mask of colorlessness. And yet there are heroes of literature who struggled titanically with their own eras—Tolstoy, Milton, Victor Hugo—who nevertheless matter more for their works than their lives.

There are great figures—Emily Dickinson, Wallace Stevens, Willa Cather—who seem to have had so little of the full intensity of life when compared to the vitality of their work, that we might almost speak of the work in the work, rather than even of the work in a person. Emily Brontë might well be the extreme instance of such a visionary, surpassing William Blake in that one regard.

I conclude this general introduction to a series of literary bio-critiques by stating a tentative formula or principle for gauging the many ways in which the work influences the person and her subsequent, later work. Our influence upon ourselves is always related to the Shakespearean invention of self-overhearing, which I have written about in several other contexts. Life, as well as poetry and prose, is overheard rather than simply heard. The writer listens to herself as though she were somebody else, and the will to change begins to operate. The forces that live in us include the prior work we have done, and the dreams and waking visions that evade our dismissals.

HAROLD BLOOM

Introduction

Toni Morrison is a novelist of extraordinary gifts. In my judgment, her principal narratives break into two clearly defined groups. The first is constituted by *The Bluest Eye* (1970), *Sula* (1973), and *Song of Solomon* (her best achievement, 1977). The second, more recent group begins with *Beloved* (1987), her most widely read work, and continues with *Jazz* (1992) and *Paradise* (1998).

It seems accurate to observe that the fictions of the second group have strong ideological overtones, reflecting Morrison's assertions that she is an African-American nationalist and a Marxist feminist, who is to be interpreted only in the context of African-American literature. *Song of Solomon* certainly has an agonistic relationship to Ralph Ellison's *Invisible Man*, but it is even closer to William Faulkner in stance and texture. And it is Virginia Woolf, stemming from English aesthetic traditions, who is the deep influence upon *The Bluest Eye* and *Sula*.

Only the judgment of time will decide the question of eminence between the earlier and later Morrison. *Jazz* and *Paradise* have their partisans, but both novels carry a heavy superstructure of political motivations that are not always consonant with their characters and events.

Beloved is certainly Morrison's most problematical work. Some readers whom I esteem set it very high, while other share my skepticism as to its aesthetic persuasiveness. It is a narrative intended to shock us into an ideological awareness, but its contrivances of plot are tendentious, and the personalities of its protagonists do not always cohere. I regard *Beloved* as a Period Piece, albeit one written by a woman of genius.

In contrast, *Song of Solomon* seems to me a permanent work. Its hero, Milkman Dead, is an authentic quester, seeking the truth of his origins. In a narrative indebted to Faulkner's *Light in August* and "The Bear," Morrison nevertheless establishes her own strong voice, and Milkman becomes an articulated person, poignant and exemplary.

ELLYN SANNA

Biography of Toni Morrison

An Unexpected Success

On a rainy autumn day in 1987, a small, gray-haired woman wearing large gold hoop earrings sat down to her lunch with a sigh of satisfaction. The rain beat against the windows of the New York City restaurant, and outside taxi horns blared, but the woman was undisturbed. "This is the first time all week they've let me have lunch," she told her companion, an editor from *The Boston Globe*. "Usually, they bring me cottage cheese."

The woman was Toni Morrison, author and writing professor, and the "they" to whom she referred was her publicity crew at Alfred A. Knopf, the company that published her books. Morrison's newest novel, *Beloved*, had just been released in September, and it made the *New York Times* bestseller list the same week it appeared in bookstores. Now, the publishing house was trying to cram as much book promotion into the short time Morrison had left before she flew to the University of California at Berkeley for four weeks as a visiting professor of creative writing and African-American studies. Morrison was forced to snatch moments of relaxation in the midst of a grueling publicity schedule. Her peaceful life had changed overnight.

When Morrison had scheduled her time at Berkeley, she had no way of knowing that her novel would become a runaway bestseller. Three weeks after its publication date, the book had climbed to number three on the bestseller list, and, after an initial print run of 100,000 copies, the novel was already in its third printing.

Toni Morrison's readership had grown steadily since the publication of her first novel, *The Bluest Eye*, in 1970, but nothing had prepared her for the way readers would take to *Beloved*. As happy as she was with the book's success, she was also tired. She had always worked hard to promote her books; "I almost felt this missionary zeal," she told the interviewer from *The Boston Globe*, "because 15 years ago a black woman novelist was 'novel.' I thought if they [the public] got accustomed to the idea, then other black women writers wouldn't have to break new ground. So I used to plow the soil, so to speak." But the hard work she put into promoting those earlier books was very different from the new fame that *Beloved* had brought her. The round of interviews and appearances was exhausting.

In fact, *Beloved* very nearly wasn't written. Morrison spent two years simply thinking about the plotline and the characters, and she took another three years to write the book. Her deadline with the publisher came before she was ready—in her mind, she had written only a third of the story—but at last, discouraged, she submitted to her editor at Knopf as much of the manuscript as she had completed. She was convinced that she had failed; the book did not live up to her expectations.

To her amazement and relief, her editor reacted with delight to what she had given him. What she considered to be only a third of the story, he told her, was actually a book in its own right. Morrison asked him repeatedly whether he was certain; he was. The novel he had just read was unusual: lyrical, almost unbearably tragic, and a masterpiece. It told the story of Sethe, a former slave who had fled the South with her children and who now lived only with her daughter Denver—and Beloved, the ghost of her other daughter, who was murdered as a baby. Although the book also explores the depths of both the mother-daughter bond and the evils of slavery, this tragedy is the mystery at the novel's center.

The idea for the story had come from an actual event that Morrison had seen reported in a 19th-century newspaper. In 1851, a slave named Margaret Garner escaped with her children from Kentucky to Ohio. Her master tracked her down, and when she was about to be captured, she tried to kill her children, apparently believing that death would be better for them than a life of slavery. Only one of the children died, and Margaret was imprisoned; but she showed no remorse for her deed. She was, she said, "unwilling to have her children suffer as she had done." She preferred to kill them quickly and end their suffering rather than to see them "taken back to slavery, and . . . murdered by piecemeal."

Toni Morrison was both intrigued and moved by this story. She did not see it as an isolated event far removed from her own world; rather, she could see parallels between Margaret Garner's life and the lives of the women around her. "What was on my mind," she told *The Boston Globe*, "was the way in which women are so vulnerable to displacing themselves, into something other than themselves. . . . There's still an enormous amount of misery and self-sabotage, and we're still shooting ourselves in the foot."

The novel's story is carried forward by the characters' voices; Morrison's genius makes these voices so real that they seem to speak aloud in the reader's mind. Toward the end of the novel, the voice of Beloved herself, the ghost girl, takes over. Morrison confesses that this character was the most difficult to create. She wanted the ghost girl to be distinct and real—not to sound like Toni Morrison.

To make Beloved come alive, Morrison got in touch with her childhood world, a world in which magic and ghosts and the supernatural were all very real. She also had to be willing to accept the pain of Beloved's world. At a distance, it is easy to dissociate oneself from the painful realities of slavery, but Morrison insists that the past be brought into the open and not repeated. When writing Beloved's story seemed too difficult, she told herself, "If they can live it, I can write about it. I refuse to believe that that period, or that thing is beyond art." To write Beloved's story was to take power from the slaveholders of the past and return it to African-Americans in general and African-American women in particular.

The result of her hard work was a book that impressed not only her editor at Knopf but millions of readers as well. In the following year, the book would win the Pulitzer Prize for fiction, and in 1998 *Beloved* would be adapted as a film, starring Oprah Winfrey as Sethe.

A Strong Sense of Identity

On February 18, 1931, Toni Morrison was born as Chloe Anthony Wofford in Lorain, Ohio, the second child of George and Ramah Willis Wofford. George and Ramah would later have two more children, making Chloe the second oldest of four.

Before Chloe's birth, the family had moved to Ohio from the South, hoping to find better employment opportunities in the less racist North. In the midst of the Great Depression, when opportunities for employment were in short supply, George Wofford took such work as he could find, including washing cars and road construction, sometimes working three jobs at once in order to provide for his family. His steadiest employment was as a shipyard welder.

Wofford was hardworking and dignified, always well dressed despite the family's poverty, and he took great pride in his work. He once told his daughter that each time he welded a perfect seam on a ship, he would sign his name to the side of the ship in welding. No one would see his name or care that it was there—but *he* knew and cared, and to him that was all that mattered.

Even though he worked diligently and well, however, Wofford sometimes had no job at all. On one occasion, when little Chloe was only two years old, the family was unable to pay the monthly rent of $4. They were evicted, but Wofford refused to leave; the family had nowhere to go. Furious, the landlord set fire to the house, with Morrison and her older sister and their parents still inside.

The family escaped unharmed, and the story became a part of the family history. Morrison was too young at the time to remember the fire, but she grew up hearing the story repeated again and again. As an adult, she realized that the incident taught her the importance of laughter. The family might have despaired when they realized how little their lives meant to the landlord; instead, they chose to laugh. Morrison's parents taught her that humor was the only way to handle some kinds of evil; she told *The Washington Post*, "That's what laughter does. You take it back. You take your life back."

George Wofford refused to let discrimination make him feel like less of a man. His pride was a treasured part of his legacy; from her father Morrison learned to appreciate her heritage. However, she also learned the negative side to her father's pride, for, like him, she was raised with a deep distrust of all white people. As a child in Georgia, her father had been shocked by the behavior of white adults, and in his adulthood his shock had turned to hatred. "My father was a racist," Toni Morrison would one day admit. He felt justified in despising all whites, and he felt that whites had no reason whatsoever to despise him.

Morrison's mother, Ramah Wofford, was also a source of strength. When African-Americans were not allowed to sit in certain sections of movie theaters, she would proudly seat herself in the "white folks' section." She was trying to prove a point to the rest of the African-American community: if she could sit there, then so could they.

Ramah refused to remain silent in the face of injustice. Once, when the family received free flour from the government, the bags were found to be full of insects. Morrison's mother immediately wrote a letter to President Franklin D. Roosevelt himself, informing him of the problem. She came from a line of women who were willing to take action, "women," Toni Morrison told *The New York Times*, "who would run *toward* the situation rather than putting someone up in front of them, or retreating."

The family may have lacked money, but in other ways it was wealthy. Stories were one part of the family treasure. Morrison grew up hearing her parents' tales of Uncle Remus, of ghosts and the supernatural. "My father's were the best, the scariest," she later told *The New York Times Magazine*. "We were always begging him to repeat the stories that terrified us most."

Tales of the supernatural were not mere stories in the family; Morrison's parents and grandparents firmly believed in the power of the spirit world. Her grandmother interpreted Morrison's dreams using a book of dream symbols, and Morrison was raised to believe the world full of omens and meaning. A ring around the moon, the presence or absence of birds, a dream about a red dress—all had significance in the minds of family members. This same sense of magic and hidden meaning would later appear in Morrison's work.

Reading was another joy in the Wofford home. Even though the family had little money, Ramah belonged to a book club, and she taught her children that books were to be treasured. Ramah's own father had attended school for only one day in his life, yet in her youth she had watched him read anything he could find. Needless to say, Morrison learned to read at an early age. When she entered the first grade, she was the only African-American child in her class—and the only child who could read.

Another blessing in the Wofford household was music. Ramah was in the church choir, and she sang as she did her housework—gospel, jazz, blues, opera. Her grandfather, John Solomon Willis, had once supported his family with his skill at the violin. Morrison was raised in a tradition and an environment of music.

Her mother's parents were the only grandparents Morrison ever knew; her father's family had died before her birth. She was very close to her grandparents, and she never felt any gap between the generations. From her grandparents, she learned what it was like to have grown up in the days of slavery. Her great-grandparents had been slaves, and her grandfather remembered hearing his parents talk about the coming "emancipation." He had not understood the word, and since his parents had often seemed upset when using it, he had feared that it was something awful. When Lincoln made his Emancipation Proclamation, Morrison's grandfather hid under a bed.

Morrison's grandparents also told her about the days when they had lived in Alabama before the move to the North. They had been sharecroppers, farming land for its owner in return for a small share in the farm's profits. The family had been very poor, and Morrison's grandfather had been forced to find supplemental work. One of those jobs had taken him to Birmingham, Alabama, where he had earned money by playing his violin.

While this grandfather was in Birmingham, his wife, Morrison's grandmother, became concerned. Her daughters were getting older, and white boys were beginning to notice them. She was afraid that trouble was coming, so she decided to leave Alabama for the North. She sent to her husband a warning that if he wanted to see his family again he must catch the midnight train with them.

She had only $18, and she had no way of knowing whether her husband had received the message. On the night of their departure, there was still no sign of Morrison's grandfather; the children burst into tears, but she herded them onto the train anyway. Only when they were on their way did her husband emerge from his hiding place. He owed money, and he was afraid someone would recognize him and not let him leave—so he had hidden until the train was about to leave the station.

Morrison's relationship with these grandparents was not only close but also often nurturing. Her grandfather became senile when she was young, often wandering and losing his way. Morrison's job was to find the old man, lead him home, settle him on the porch, and offer him walnuts. When her grandmother was dying, it was the little girl's duty to read the Bible to her. Performing these tasks fostered in Morrison a sense of belonging to a cycle of generations—which in turn helped her to understand her own identity.

Growing up in a world in which prejudice and discrimination were facts of life, Morrison needed this strong self-concept. Her family lived in an integrated neighborhood, and she went to school with children of a variety of ethnic backgrounds—but there were certain lines that African-Americans were not supposed to cross. They were barred from some places in the town, including the lake in the town park in which white children were allowed to swim. Sometimes, the discrimination was pointed directly at Morrison instead of at the African-American community in general. For instance, a group of older white boys often threw stones at the girl and her friends and called them names. Morrison was afraid of the boys, but she also felt scornful; why would fourteen-year-old boys feel they needed to attack six-year-old girls of half their size?

When the outside world was hostile, though, Morrison knew she could rely on her own family. Each member had his or her own responsibilities within the family framework, and each knew she or he could count on the others. When Morrison was told to ensure that supper didn't burn, she took her job seriously; she knew that if the food *did* burn then there would be nothing to replace it and the entire family would go hungry.

When Morrison was 12 years old, her responsibilities expanded; she was sent to earn money to supplement the family's income. In the following year, when she was 13, she began cleaning for a white family. One day she came home and complained to her father that the white woman was cruel and the work too hard. She later told *Newsweek* that her father answered, "Girl, you don't live there. You live *here*. So you go do your work, get your money, and come on home." His words reinforced yet again a lesson her family had taught her over and over: she did not have to let other people determine how she felt about herself.

Family was not the only influence on Morrison's early life; her neighborhood, a community of other African-Americans, also played a significant role in her upbringing. These people, too, took their responsibility to each other seriously: if a member of the community was ill, they took care of that person; they provided what food they could if a family had nothing; and they took turns caring for those who were too old to care for themselves. They also kept a sharp eye on the children. "They meddled in your lives a lot," Toni Morrison later told *The Massachusetts Review*. "They felt that you belonged to them. And every woman on the street could raise everybody's child, and tell you exactly what to do and you felt that connection with those people and they felt it with you. And when they punished us or hollered at us, it was, at the time, we thought, so inhibiting and so cruel, and it's only later that you realize that they were interested in you. Interested in you—they cared about your behavior."

Morrison grew up understanding that when these women called each other "sister" they truly meant it. The connections within the neighborhood were profound, and as an adult Morrison would realize that the closeness had been life-giving, helping her to feel both safe and important. At the time, though, Morrison was eager to distance herself from her neighbors' watchful eyes.

She did well in high school, where she was a member of the National Honor Society, and she loved to read; her favorites were Tolstoy, Dostoyevsky, Flaubert, Austen, Hemingway, Faulkner, and Cather. As an African-American, she did not identify easily with the characters in these authors' works; but she savored their well-chosen words anyway. Despite her love of books, she had no idea of becoming a writer herself. Instead, she hoped to become a dancer, like her favorite ballerina, Maria Tallchief.

In 1949, she was graduated with honors from the Lorain high school. Her achieving graduation at all was a momentous event in her family; her father had never managed as much, and only one uncle had gone to college. But the members of the family had always done whatever was necessary in order to survive, and Morrison knew, as her family did, that in order to support herself she would need a skill. Also, she also was eager to leave her hometown and see the world outside Lorain.

A New Name

For the previous 17 years, Morrison's father had held down three jobs at once, and now he had saved enough money to send his daughter to prestigious Howard University in Washington, D.C., where Morrison studied English and the classics.

Although the students at Howard were predominantly African-American, Morrison was disappointed to find that her classes offered her few opportunities to study the writings of African-American authors. Instead, the curriculum focused on white male authors, such as Shakespeare, Hawthorne, and Melville. Morrison had already read the work of these authors, and she found herself becoming bored.

She also soon tired of the social life on campus. Clothing and parties were more important to many of the students than were ideas and feelings, and a person's popularity depended largely on her wealth; Morrison had learned very different values from her own family and community. Her peers at Howard couldn't even pronounce her name correctly, so while she was there she became known as Toni, a shortened form of her middle name. She liked her new name—but she still felt out of place and generally bored.

What saved her during her four years at Howard was her involvement in the Howard University Players, a traveling acting company. She had heard countless stories from her family of what it was like to be a black person in the Southern states, but while traveling with the Players she at last saw this life for herself. What she saw made a lasting impression on her, and 15 years later, when she began to write, she would make use of the sights and sounds and smells she experienced on those acting tours. Because the audiences were completely segregated, though—i.e. made up only of African-Americans—Morrison was never exposed to the racial violence that her father had fled the South to escape.

Morrison left Howard University in 1953 with a bachelor's degree in English. She then attended Cornell University, where she received a master's degree in English in 1955. Morrison was ready for her career now—but she wasn't sure just what that would be. "I was partly drawn to teaching," she told *The Chicago Tribune*, "because I didn't know what to do with a master's in English." She accepted a position teaching introductory English at Texas Southern University in Houston.

To her surprise and delight, she loved her new job. She also enjoyed the emphasis Texas Southern placed on African-American culture. At Howard University, black culture had mostly been ignored or downplayed; Morrison's new campus did not look at African-American traditions as merely a personal or family matter but treated them as a discipline in their own right.

In 1957, however, Morrison decided to return to Howard University to teach English. There she met Harold Morrison, a Jamaican architect; they were married in the following year, and it was then that her name completed its transformation from Chloe Wofford to Toni Morrison.

During these years, the Civil Rights Movement was beginning to spread from campus to campus across the country. Morrison had the chance to meet many of the people who would later be leaders in this movement—Amiri Baraka, then called LeRoi Jones, and Andrew Young, who would later work with Martin Luther King Jr. and later yet become the mayor of Atlanta. One of Morrison's students was Stokely Carmichael, who became a leader of the Student Nonviolent Coordinating Committee, and another was Claude Brown, who went on to become a noted African-American author.

Morrison herself was not deeply involved with the Civil Rights Movement, though. She was too busy with her personal life to have much time for politics—especially after 1961, when her son, Harold Ford, was born.

Morrison continued teaching, though, even while she cared for her new family. Her marriage was not proving to be a happy one; the cultural differences between Morrison and her Jamaican husband were too great to be overcome easily. As she later told *The New York Times*, "Women in Jamaica . . . never challenge their husbands. I was a constant nuisance to mine. He didn't need me making judgments about him, which I did. A lot."

Morrison and her husband faced other differences as well, and she joined a writers' group as a way to escape temporarily from the pressures she faced at home. She had never considered producing her own work, but she craved the company of others who felt as she did about reading.

The ten writers in the group, most of them poets, met once a month to discuss one another's writing. Each member was to present an original story at every meeting. At first, Morrison simply used stories she had written in high school, but she soon ran out of these. When she had nothing left to take to the next meeting, she dashed off a story about someone she had known back in Lorain, Ohio, a little African-American girl who had prayed to God for blue eyes.

The girl had told Morrison that she no longer believed in God; despite all her prayers, He had never given her the blue eyes she asked for. Even at the time, Morrison thought it was a good thing the girl's prayers were not answered. She knew that even though the other child could not see it, she was beautiful just the way she was. The story she wrote based on this girl was full of pain; because the little girl had no sense of her own beauty, she was a victim of everything and everyone around her. The writers' group liked her story, but Morrison did not give it any further thought.

In 1964, pregnant with her second child, Morrison decided to resign her teaching position at Howard University. She and her husband took young Ford to Europe for the summer. The time away did nothing to improve their relationship, though, and while they were in Europe the Morrisons separated.

Eventually, they were divorced. Harold Morrison returned to Jamaica, and Toni Morrison returned to her family in Ohio, where she bore her second son, Slade Kevin Morrison. She had two children to support and no job; Morrison's future looked bleak. She knew her family would take care of her if necessary, but she didn't want to be dependent on anyone. She wanted to find independence, her own identity—to learn whether she was strong enough to live life on her own.

A New Passion

In the next year, 1965, Morrison saw her chance to become independent. In *The New York Review of Books*, she found an advertisement for an editorial position with the textbook subsidiary of Random House in Syracuse, New York. Morrison was certain that she could do the job.

Random House hired her as an associate editor, and Morrison and her two young sons moved to Syracuse, where Morrison knew no one. The year and a half she spent there was lonely and lackluster, but three events of the time later stood out in her mind. The first was hiring a white housekeeper to take care of her sons while she worked. As a young teenager, Morrison had done the same work in a white household; the role reversal pleased her.

Another event was extremely *un*pleasant. A neighbor in her apartment building complained about the noise Morrison's sons made. As the argument between Morrison and the other woman escalated, the woman called Morrison a "tramp." Morrison did nothing but go to work and come home to care for her children; she had no time for other relationships, and she fiercely resented the woman's insult. Furious, she took the woman to court, although she eventually dropped her case.

The third of the occurrences that mark her time in Syracuse, though, would alter the course of her life. In that first lonely, snowy winter, after her sons were in bed, she took up once again her story about the girl who wanted blue eyes—and, drawing on both her memories and her imagination, she added to it. She found the story's characters became more exciting and fascinating to her than anything else in her life, with the exception of her sons, and writing to be the most challenging and fulfilling task she had ever undertaken. For the first time, Morrison wrote seriously.

The Bluest Eye, the novel she was creating, tells the story of the abused Pecola Breedlove, a girl on the brink of adolescence who, finding validation nowhere in her life, becomes obsessed with the winning good looks of a child celebrity, praying so hard for blue eyes that she finally comes to believe she has them. Night after night, while her children slept, Morrison threw herself into Pecola's story.

She hoped to be transferred to New York City soon, so she saw no point in making friends in Syracuse; as a result, she had no social life. Without Pecola's story, Morrison would have had nothing to do after she put her sons to bed. At first she wrote simply, as a means of passing time; but soon her writing became more important to her than her work at Random House. She had no idea whether the story would ever be published; rather, she wrote because she wanted to find out what happened next. She later told an editor at *The New York Times*, "Writing was for me the most extraordinary way of thinking and feeling. It became the one thing I was doing that I had absolutely no intention of living without."

In 1967, Random House did transfer Morrison to New York City, where she became a senior editor. She began working on books by African-American writers like Muhammad Ali, Angela Davis, and Andrew Young. Meanwhile, though, Morrison was also trying to find a publisher for her own novel, which she had now completed.

She worried that Random House would disapprove of her writing a book of her own, so she submitted the book to other publishers in secret. At last, in 1970, the novel was published.

Morrison had intended to use her birth name on the book, but instead the name Toni Morrison appeared on the cover. This was the name by which Morrison's editor knew her; no one had thought to verify that this was the name under which she wanted to be published. By the time Morrison realized what had happened, it was too late; she would be known as Toni Morrison from that point onward.

The Bluest Eye was not a success in sales, but it was reviewed in many well-known publications—*The New York Times Book Review*, *Newsweek*, *The New Yorker*, and *The Chicago Tribune* among them—and the critics all agreed that it was an astonishing first novel. They particularly praised Morrison's poetic use of language.

Morrison was pleased by the critical acclaim, but she did not like to have her words considered "poetic." Her goal had not been to create a fancy, self-conscious piece of writing; instead, she had wanted to write as real people spoke. The white reviewers, however, were not familiar with African-American dialects. "It's always seemed to me," Morrison said in an interview with *The New York Times Book Review*, "that black people's grace has been with what they do with language."

The critics also liked Morrison's sympathetic portrayals of "evil" people like Pecola Breedlove's father. In the *New York Times Book Review* article on *The Bluest Eye*, Haskel Frankel commented, "There are many novelists willing to report the ugliness of the world as ugly. The writer who can reveal the beauty and the hope beneath the surface is a writer to seek out and encourage."

Morrison *was* encouraged. Because of the recognition she received for *The Bluest Eye*, publications began to turn to her as an authority on African-American culture. In the next two years, Morrison wrote 28 book reviews for these publications. She also wrote an essay for *The New York Times Magazine* on Women's Liberation. Morrison's essay pointed out that the movement did little to help poor women of color.

Morrison still did not see herself as a novelist; she had written one book, and at this point she had no plans to write another. Slowly, though, she realized that something was missing from her life. She felt sad and restless; the characters of *The Bluest Eye* had been her constant companions for years, and now she missed them.

Perhaps as a replacement, a new character began to take shape in her mind.

The Nature of Evil

Morrison's new character was a "bad" woman who did exactly what she wanted, with no thought of what people would think of her. After this woman became real to her, Morrison found herself wondering what it would be like if this woman had a friend of just the opposite personality.

Sula, Toni Morrison's second novel, focused on the friendship between these two African-American women, conservative Nel Wright and scandalous Sula Peace. Until then, no one had ever created a novel that centered on the friendship between two women. Morrison explained later, in an interview with Paula Giddings from *Encore American & Worldwide News*, "People talk about the friendship of women, and them having respect for each other, like it's something new. But Black women have always had that, they always have been emotional life supports for each other."

Morrison wrote the book in her head on the subway between her home in Queens and her job in Manhattan. It took another two and a half years to produce the story on paper; her attention was being drawn into other directions. In 1971, she had accepted a position as a visiting professor of English at the State University of New York at Purchase. At the same time, she continued to work as an editor for Random House. Teaching, editing, writing book reviews, and raising her sons left Morrison little time in which to write a novel.

Sometimes, Morrison felt overwhelmed by all her responsibilities. Then one day she sat down and made a list of all the things she had to accomplish—and she made a second list of the things she truly *wanted* to accomplish. She discovered that she could live without many of the things that had been occupying her time. The only two things she could not live without were her sons and her fiction.

With her priorities clarified, Morrison made time for writing by cutting out much of her social life. She no longer went out with friends or entertained, and she kept her time on the telephone to a minimum. Ironically, at a time when she was writing a story about friendship, she had little room for friendship in her own life. She knew that in order to succeed as both a writer and a single mother she would have to regulate her life carefully. While her hands were occupied with housework, or anything else that didn't claim her whole attention, she composed her stories.

Her greatest challenge, though, was finding time for both of her priorities, her children and her writing. She found that, even when she tried to write in seclusion, her sons distracted her; she was constantly losing her train of thought because of their interruptions. At last, though, she discovered that when she worked and they played in the same room they interrupted her work far less. They were content as long as she was there where they could see her, and she slowly learned to concentrate despite their noise. She dedicated *Sula* to her two sons.

In some ways, the novel was a success. Sara Blackburn of *The New York Times* wrote that Toni Morrison's "dialogue is so compressed and life-like that it sizzles. . . . it's hard to believe we haven't known [the characters] forever." The book became an alternate selection of the Book-of-the-Month Club, and excerpts from it were published in *Redbook*. In 1975, *Sula* was nominated for the National Book Award for fiction.

But not everyone liked *Sula*. Some reviewers balked at Morrison's unusual characters. But she was drawn to people who were eccentric and colorful; in real life, they were the people who fascinated her, and they were the characters she wanted to write about. Other critics complained about still another aspect of Morrison's writing: they didn't like the way she wrote about violence and evil in *Sula*.

The book tells the story of Nel and Sula's friendship from childhood until almost half a century later. As girls, their differences enrich their relationship, but as adults those same differences lead them in opposite directions. Nel marries young and has a family, and Sula lives mysteriously away from their hometown. When Sula returns, she sleeps with other women's husbands, including Nel's. The community perceives Sula as evil but does nothing to stop her. Morrison explained the community's attitude in an interview with Thomas LeClair of *The New Republic*: "In the black community where I grew up, there were eccentricity and freedom. . . . people did anything and nobody was run out of town. I mean, the community in *Sula* let her stay. . . . They protected themselves from her, but she was a part of the community."

Some readers were uncomfortable with this live-and-let-live attitude toward scandalous behavior. They pointed to particularly violent scenes in the book—the young Sula's watching her mother burn to death, for example, or Sula's grandmother's killing of her own son. Morrison's narration recounts these scenes amorally, and her matter-of-fact, nonjudgemental approach concerned some reviewers. Jerry H. Bryant wrote in *The Nation* that Morrison and writers like her were "slowly, subtly making our old buildings unsafe. . . . There is something ominous in the chilling detachment with which they view their characters."

Morrison's response to these critics was that they didn't understand the African-American community. She had intended *Sula* to treat the problem of good and evil, but she wasn't viewing these concepts as white people did. African-Americans' perception of evil fascinated her. In *Black Women Writers at Work*, Claudia Tate quotes Morrison:

> It was interesting to me that black people at one time seemed not to respond to evil in the ways other people did, but that they thought evil had a natural place in the universe; they did not wish to eradicate it. They just wished to protect themselves from it, maybe even manipulate it, but they never wanted to kill it. They thought evil was just another aspect of life. The ways black people dealt with evil accounted in my mind for how they responded to a lot of other things. It's like a double-edged sword. It accounts for one of the reasons it's difficult for them to organize long-term political wars against another people. It accounts for their generosity and acceptance of all sorts of things. It's because they're not terrified by evil, by difference. Evil is not an alien force; it's just a different force. That's the evil I was describing in *Sula*.

The literary world was used to works that were built on the foundation of Western philosophy, a binary or dichotomous worldview that pitted the light against darkness, good against evil, always in opposed pairs. Morrison's strong sense of identity gave her the courage to write another kind of book; her writing was firmly based on the African-American tradition, an entirely different way of looking at the world.

Despite the good reviews that *Sula* did receive, many readers agreed with the critics; they were uncomfortable with Toni Morrison's unique slant on reality. Like *The Bluest Eye*, *Sula* was not a success financially.

For the time being, Morrison decided not to write another novel. Instead, she focused on a different project that was almost as important to her.

NEW CHALLENGES

"Anything I have ever learned of any consequence, I have learned from Black people," Toni Morrison told Betty Jean Parker in an interview included in *Sturdy Black Bridges*. "I have never been bored by *any* Black person, ever.... I am like a painter who is preoccupied with painting violins, and may never do moods or paint a tree."

Toni Morrison loved her legacy of African-American history and tradition; she believed it was one of the richest and most beautiful that the world had to offer. She wanted to share African-American history with the rest of the world.

The Black Book was designed to do just that. It was a scrapbook put out by Random House that covered 300 years of African-American history. Toni Morrison's name would not appear on the book, but the project was her idea, and she spent a year and a half working on it. The book was different from most other history books, for Morrison made sure that it was told from the point of view of ordinary people.

Because she felt so strongly that the book's voice should come from everyday African-Americans, rather than from professional writers, Morrison worked with Middleton A. ("Spike") Harris, a retired New York State parole officer, and three other contributors—Morris Levitt, Roger Furman, and Ernest Smith. These were the names that would be listed on the title page as the book's contributors.

Under Morrison's supervision, these men organized a collection of old newspaper clippings, photographs, patent-office records, song lyrics, advertisements, and selections from slave narratives. Morrison also asked her own family and friends to submit material; her cousin recorded the story of the family's flight from the South. The book covered nearly every aspect of African-American history, including sections on voodoo and on the interpretation of dreams. *The Black Book* was published in 1974.

Meanwhile, Morrison had moved out of the city into the suburbs. This meant that she had to make a daily 45-minute drive to her job in Manhattan. Her sons rode with her; every morning at 8:00, before she went to work, she dropped them off at the United Nations International School in Manhattan. She retrieved them at 3:30 in the afternoon, and they all drove home again. She didn't ask Random House for permission to follow this schedule.

She followed the same philosophy when she was offered a teaching position at Yale University in 1977. On Fridays, she taught classes on the technique of fiction and the writings of African-American women—and the other four days of the week she continued to work as an editor at Random House. "I didn't ask anyone's permission to be out of the office on Fridays," Morrison told Colette Dowling in an interview for *The New York Times Magazine*. "I simply took the job. One day my boss announced that there'd be a production meeting or something on the following Friday. 'I won't be there,' I told him. 'I teach at Yale on Fridays.'"

As busy as she was, she still found time for her writing. In 1977, her third novel, *Song of Solomon*, was published. *Solomon* tells the story of a boy called Milkman—given the name because his mother had nursed him for years. His father, a cruel landlord, is the richest man in their community. When Milkman is 12 years old, his Aunt Pilate comes to visit. Pilate is like no one Milkman has ever met before: she carries a bag of human bones, wears a brass box in one ear, practices voodoo, sells bootleg whiskey; and lives in a dilapidated shack. Milkman's father has always rejected his family's history, but through Pilate Milkman begins to appreciate the family's rich and eccentric legacy.

The stories of *Sula* and *Beloved* were firmly anchored to one small community, based on the town of Morrison's birth, but in *Song of Solomon* Morrison allowed her character to leave his home. Milkman travels in search of a bag of gold from his family's past, and his journey takes him from his home in Michigan to Pennsylvania and then south to Virginia. Instead of finding gold, however, Milkman discovers another sort of treasure: his own family's history, including the story of his great-grandfather Solomon, who is said to have literally flown away from slavery.

Morrison used the metaphor of flight throughout *Song of Solomon* to underscore another difference between this book and her two earlier novels: *Song of Solomon* was about men instead of women. Women, Morrison said, have traditionally lived in small, enclosed worlds; their attention turns inward. Men, on the other hand, focus on the world around them. As she commented in an interview for *The New York Times Book Review*, "black men travel, they split, they get on trains, they walk, they move."

In *Song of Solomon*, Toni Morrison also wanted to explore the theme of physical flight that runs through so many African-American folktales. "Flying was one of our gifts," she told Thomas LeClair of *The New Republic*. "I don't care how silly it may seem. It is everywhere—people used to talk about it, it's in the spirituals and gospels. Perhaps it was wishful thinking—escape, death, and all that. But suppose it wasn't. What might it mean? I tried to find out in *Song of Solomon*." Flight, says Morrison, is a part of African-American life, a "positive, majestic thing," but it comes with a price: the man who flies away leaves someone behind, usually a child. The flight becomes a part of the family mythology, but so does abandonment.

Writing from a man's perspective was difficult for Morrison. She struggled to find new ways of thinking and writing. She drew on her close relationship with her sons, using their reactions and emotions to help her to understand how a male protagonist would act. "I learned a lot from my sons," she told *Newsweek*, "seeing how excited they got by going near danger for instance—they'd come away *charged*, lifted, as if somebody'd turned the volume up."

But her relationship with her sons also added tension to the time when she was working on *Song of Solomon*. Her sons were growing, and being a single mother now presented new challenges. Ford, the older of the two, was in the middle of his adolescence; Morrison told *The Washington Post*, "My eldest son was entering manhood and if they do that properly, they do it explosively." She paused and then joked, "He was doing it properly."

But Morrison was not to be intimidated. She acknowledged that the ideal way to raise children would be with two parents, but she refused to resent her own circumstances. Instead, she took pride in taking charge of her own life—and that included raising her sons alone.

Soon, though, tragedy rendered her work on *Solomon* even more difficult: her father, who had inspired and challenged her all her life, died. Morrison's grief threatened to overwhelm her, but she discovered that writing could help her to cope with the loss. In her interview with Paula Giddings, Morrison said, "I think because I was so depressed, my defenses were down. I wasn't fighting anything. And it was like a gate that opened in me. I began to envision the things in the book. I started writing and writing—I think I wrote 30 pages that night." Morrison allowed her pain to connect her with the creative voice inside her—and when it did, she found that writing offered her healing and hope.

Even though her father was dead, she had long conversations with him in her mind. She felt that his wisdom was still helping and encouraging her. The dedication of *Song of Solomon* consists of a single word: "Daddy."

After Morrison finished *Song of Solomon*, she mentioned to her editor that she was considering working less as an editor so that she would have more time for writing. He told her she should make up her mind about what she wanted to be "when she grew up"—an editor or a writer. His joking comment took Morrison by surprise. Until then, she had never considered that she might be able to make her living writing. As a single parent, she had taken for granted that she would always have to work, supporting herself and her sons by teaching and editing. It had never occurred to her that her income from writing might suffice.

Now, for the first time, she decided to concentrate fully on writing. Even before she knew how well *Song of Solomon* would sell, she resigned from her position at Random House. She wanted to risk a firm commitment to writing. She did agree to edit four or five books a year for Random House; she felt she had a responsibility to other African-American writers, and she wanted to help them to see their work published.

Song of Solomon proved successful; for the first time, one of Morrison's books not only was favored by the critics, but also sold well. *The New York Times Book Review* featured it on its front page, and *Redbook* published it as a serial. The book was also a main selection of the Book-of-the-Month Club, making Toni Morrison the first African-American to receive that recognition since Richard Wright's *Native Son* in 1940. *Song of Solomon* also won the National Book Critics Circle Award for fiction in 1977. When the book was released as a paperback, it became a bestseller.

Morrison's new success didn't seem quite real to her until, one day, as she was driving aimlessly, passing time while her son was at a piano lesson, she noticed a display for *Song of Solomon* in a bookstore window. A huge sign called the book "A Triumph by Toni Morrison." Morrison realized what she had achieved.

With the money the novel brought her, Morrison bought a boathouse in upstate New York, on the Hudson River. The house had a private dock and an expansive porch where Morrison could sit in a wooden swing and write. When she had first seen the house, looking out at the river she had felt her father's presence beside her. She had been certain he was telling her she should buy the house.

Her new home was only 30 minutes from her job in Manhattan, but now Morrison worked at Random House only one day a week. Her sons were transferred to a local public school, and the family no longer had to make its arduous daily commute.

The only drawback to Morrison's new success was her family's reaction back in Ohio. She discovered that now, when she returned home, the people she had grown up with saw her differently. They were so impressed with her accomplishments that they could only stare. The women who had once told her how to run her life now were silent and shy.

MIXED REVIEWS

After the publication of *Song of Solomon,* Morrison began work on her fourth novel, *Tar Baby.* The book was based on the well-known Uncle Remus story of Brer Rabbit and the Tar Baby, a story Morrison had heard as a child, in which Brer Rabbit, haplessly stuck to an object of tar left for him by a wily farmer, tricks the farmer into throwing him into a briar patch, whose thorns he uses to free himself—finally fleeing "lickety-split," shouting, "This is where I was born and bred."

For some reason, despite its happy ending, the story terrified Morrison as a child. As an adult, she saw the story in a new light. "It's a love story, really," she told Mel Watkins in an interview for *The New York Times Book Review.* "[T]he tar baby is a black woman; the rabbit is a black man, the powerless, clever creature who has to outwit his master. He is determined to live in that briar patch, even though he has the option to stay with her and live comfortably, securely, without touching the borders of his life. Do you think she would go into that briar patch with him? Well, that's what it's all about. If there is any consistent theme in my fiction, I guess that's it—how and why we learn to live this life intensely and well."

Morrison labored over *Tar Baby* for four and a half years. Sometimes she would write day and night for three days in a row—and at other times a week or two would pass without a word. During those long stretches when she could not or did not write, she continued to think about the story; she understood that she needed to be patient and wait for the next piece of the story to come to her. She used the days when she felt "blocked" to attend to the rest of her life—fortunately, for when she was busy writing she sometimes forgot everything else. She would become so deeply immersed in her story that she even forgot to keep appointments.

The book finally was published, to mixed reviews, and it sold well. One month after its publication, it made the *New York Times* bestseller list, and it stayed there for 16 weeks. Morrison helped to promote her book by making a tour of 14 cities, signing books and granting interviews, including one to NBC's *Today Show.* The book's best publicity, though, came from Morrison's appearance on the cover of *Newsweek.* Morrison was the second African-American woman—Zora Neale Hurston being the first, in 1943—ever to achieve that distinction.

Many reviewers praised *Tar Baby,* but others said that Morrison's poetic prose and snappy dialogue were overdone. They felt she had pushed her language too far, making it seem artificial. As John Irving explained in *The New York Times Book Review*, "A novelist's vice usually resembles his virtue, for what he does best he also tends to do to excess."

Other critics said the book was too political. Morrison disagreed; she did not think *Tar Baby* was any more political than any of her other books. The difference, she felt, was that in *Tar Baby*, for the first time, she directed her story at white readers as well as African-Americans. The politics in her earlier books had been directed only at other blacks, and so, she said, whites had not been offended. In *Tar Baby*, though, Morrison portrayed the harsh conflicts between the races. One of the book's characters goes so far as to say, "White folks and black folks should not sit down and eat together or do any of those personal things in life."

Morrison's ethnic background became a major issue during her publicity tour for *Tar Baby*. She was sometimes angry with reviewers who commented on her race. She felt strongly that being black should not be looked on as a disadvantage for an author, and she fiercely resented the implication that an African-American author might not be taken as seriously as any other. On the other hand, however, she clearly defined herself as an African-American writer; she was proud of her heritage, and she was not afraid to publicize that pride. "When they say I'm a great American novelist," she told the interviewer from *The Boston Globe*, "I say, 'Ha! They're trying to say I'm not black.' When they say I'm a wonderful woman novelist, I think 'Aha, they think I don't belong.' So I've just insisted—insisted!—upon being called a black woman novelist. And *I* decided what that meant. . . . As a black and a woman, I have had access to a range of emotions and perceptions that were unavailable to people who were neither." Morrison knew that a white male could never have written the novels she had—and she took pride in that fact. She wanted her unique identity as an author to be recognized as an advantage.

Morrison's awareness of racism was fundamental to her identity, both as an individual and as an author. In a speech she delivered at an international library congress in New York in 1986, she said, "Had I lived the life that the state planned for me from the beginning, I would have lived and died in somebody else's kitchen, or somebody else's land, and never written a word. That knowledge is bone deep, and it informs everything I do."

The Problem of Racism

If white readers had sometimes cringed at the criticism implied in *Tar Baby*, they had even more to deal with when they went to see Morrison's first play, *Dreaming Emmett*, first performed on January 4, 1986, in honor of the first national celebration of Martin Luther King Jr.'s birthday.

Dreaming Emmett was based on an actual incident. Emmett Till was a 14-year-old African-American boy who in 1955 traveled from his home in Chicago to stay with his uncle in Mississippi. During his visit, Emmett and his cousins entered a store to buy bubble gum. After their purchase, Emmett politely said goodbye to the woman behind the counter, but once they were outside, one of his cousins told him, "Hey, don't you know you're not supposed to say goodbye to a white woman?" Before Emmett could answer, another cousin commented on how pretty the woman had been, and Emmett let out a whistle of agreement.

Some white men playing poker outside the store overheard this innocent exchange. On the following Sunday, in the early hours of the morning, an armed group of white men, including the store clerk's husband, took Emmett to a plantation 25 miles away and beat him; three days later, Emmett's body was found in a nearby river, so mutilated that Emmett's mother had to identify him by a ring he wore. His accused murderers were brought to trial, but an all-white male jury found them not guilty—and the verdict became one of the sparks that eventually ignited the Civil Rights Movement.

Morrison added details from her own imagination. She used Emmett Till's death to discuss the high incidence of violent death among African-American young men. She told *The New York Times*, "There are these young black men getting shot all over the country today, not because they were stealing but because they're black. And no one remembers how any of them looked. No one even remembers the facts of each case."

Writing the story as a play instead of a novel had not been easy. In a novel, Morrison was in complete control, while a play required the input and interpretation of other artists. She had always welcomed a new challenge, though—and despite her awareness that no other writer had ever successfully made the transition from novels to plays she was confident that her skill with dialogue would help her to succeed.

Besides, Morrison was already familiar with the theater. Her college experiences in the traveling acting troupe served as a foundation, and since then she had written the lyrics for a musical, *New Orleans*, for performance as a workshop production at the Public Theater in Manhattan. Recently, she had also completed the screenplay for *Tar Baby*.

Nor did Morrison have to depend on her own talents alone. The play was directed by one of her friends, Gilbert Moses. Moses had already directed two segments of the television miniseries *Roots*, and his skill combined with Morrison's to produce a powerful play.

In *Emmett*, the characters and the action shift back and forth in time and place. At the center of the play is an African-American boy murdered 30 years before. Dreaming, he summons up his murderers, his family, and his friends—but these ghosts refuse to be controlled by his imagination. All see the past from their own perspectives. The idea for the play came to her, Morrison said, because she wanted to "see a collision of three or four levels of time through the eyes of one person who could come back to life and seek vengeance."

The play universalizes Emmett Till's murder, claims it as a part of the cultural heritage of every American, regardless of race. Morrison draws no simple or absolute conclusions. As one of the play's sponsors said, "There are no good guys or bad guys. . . . The text deals with layer of human experience in human terms rather than in philosophical or abstract terms." Another sponsor commented, "Morrison has been able to take one of the toughest themes, child murder, and make it the subject of a retrospective history. It puts Till's death in a totally different context."

Dreaming Emmett won the New York State Governor's Art Award, and it received good reviews. Margaret Croyden wrote in *The New York Times*, "Toni Morrison's voice has been a powerful one in literature. Those working with her on *Dreaming Emmett* feel that she will now also be a powerful theatrical voice." But Morrison had laid aside a book project to work on the play, and now she turned back to her novels.

She wanted to write a book that would explore the fundamental cause of racism in America—slavery. Writing this book was something Morrison felt she needed to do; she wanted to understand how a woman could absorb and cope with a reality so terrible as to be almost beyond comprehension. Yet Morrison was reluctant to write about slavery. When she wrote a novel, she was totally immersed in the story—and she did not want to lose herself in the horror of the Southern past. She did not want to force herself to remember.

She recognized that she knew very little about slavery. Even the span of time slavery had endured—300 years—was overwhelming to her. But she did not want to write about the institution, the facts and statistics; instead, she wanted to bring to life the real individuals who had lived and died as slaves.

She began her research and found that America had whitewashed its memory of slavery. Even slave museums, she realized, tended to focus on the periphery of the life, such as the quilts slaves had made, rather than on the dreadful conditions the slaves had endured. White Americans weren't the only ones who wanted to forget this grim aspect of U.S. history, she found; African-Americans didn't want to be reminded of slavery, either.

Finally, she began to read the diaries of plantation owners, and she also went to Brazil to do research. She found that the Brazilians' slave museums were far more honest on the subject.

In a diary, she read the words of one slave owner who described putting a bit on his slave Jenny 19 times in six months—the bit being a kind of metal tongue that made speech impossible in such a way as to leave the mouth sore even two days after the device's removal. Another woman had been made to wear a bell, so that her owner could hear her wherever she went. Slaves who cut sugarcane were made to wear masks to keep them from eating the crop; the masks were so hot that when they were removed the skin often came with them. These devices were not intended as instruments of torture; at the time they were ways to control a slave's behavior while she worked. To Morrison, this made the practice even more dreadful; the slave owners had totally failed to recognize their slaves' humanity.

She wanted to write about the people who suffered such inhumane treatment, so that her readers would understand that slaves were not something "other," something different and alien from the rest of humanity; she wanted them to know that these hideous things had happened to real human beings—to give the victims names.

But before she could even begin a novel about slavery, Morrison needed to get inside the experience. She used her imagination to understand what it would feel like to have no control over her future, to be separated from her family, to see her children taken from her and sold to other plantations. Slavery could no longer be a subject she avoided. Now she made it her own, as though this experience had happened to her and her own children. She spent three years thinking about her novel, and it would take her another three to write it.

A MEMORIAL

The idea for this novel, Morrison's fifth, had come to her during production of *The Black Book*. While collecting material, she had come across a newspaper article written in 1856 that told the story of Margaret Garner, mentioned earlier, who had tried to kill her children rather than allow them to be returned to slavery. *Beloved* is not told chronologically; instead, it jumps back and forth between past and present as the characters share their memories. Sometimes these characters have different versions of the same event, but together they put together a picture of slavery's reality.

When the dead child, Beloved, comes back, reincarnated in the body of a young woman, she too has memories to share. Her memories are not only her own, though, but those of all her ancestors, including the Africans who died on the ship to the New World.

Morrison felt that these people needed to be remembered and recognized, but she could find little record of the journey from Africa to America. The slaves seemed not even to have handed down stories orally, from generation to generation, as they had of other events.

Morrison turned to the diaries of slave-ship captains. Perhaps as way to handle their guilt, these men had often felt compelled to write of the hideous events they had witnessed and in which they had participated. Morrison read that slave ships had experienced difficulty in navigating the Congo River in Africa because the river was so jammed with bodies, the corpses of Africans who had been captured by slave traders and then died before they could even leave the continent. The slave traders assumed that at least half of their human cargo would die on every trip; if they were asked to deliver 400 slaves, they would pack 800.

Most small towns in the South have a monument to a Confederate hero. "But there's not one memorial or haven or park dedicated to slaves," Toni Morrison pointed out in an interview with *Newsweek*. She dedicated *Beloved* to the 60 million Africans who never even survived the voyage to America. She wanted her book to be a memorial to them.

The book was considered a literary success, and it was a commercial success as well. But more than anything else, it served as a powerful reminder of slavery's reality. Many readers for the first time understood that slavery was as hideous a scar on human history as was the Holocaust. Morrison's powerful writing pulled readers into the lives of slaves, enabling readers to claim the slaves' tragic memories as their own. A reviewer for *The New Leader* summarized, "Being one with people who were not regarded as people, we learn what living intensely means, and we will never be the same again."

Because Morrison saw herself as both an African-American author *and* a female author, in *Beloved* she wanted to deal with another issue besides race: the nature of a woman's love. Morrison told *The Southern Review*, "A woman loved something other than herself so much. She had placed all of the value of her life in something outside herself. . . . [T]he woman who killed her children loved her children so much; they were the best part of her and she would not see them sullied." The quality of a woman's love was still the same today, Morrison concluded. And it was this fine and noble quality, a woman's best attribute, that also made women sabotage themselves. Women, Morrison said, never see their own lives as being worthy of protection. By always putting their love for others ahead of any love they might have for themselves, ultimately they lose their own sense of who they are. They destroy themselves, *their* selves. Love can compel them to break rules.

Still, Morrison asserts, no one has the right to judge a woman for killing her child out of love; only her dead child can judge her. In Morrison's novel, the girl Beloved is both that child and the self that women have denied for centuries. Beloved's reactions and feelings are the story's heart.

Although most reviewers praised *Beloved*, some were uncomfortable with Beloved's reincarnation. These critics felt that Morrison's book was asking readers to suspend their disbelief of such an unlikely event without helping them to do so. They criticized Morrison for a clumsy blurring of the edge between fantasy and reality. Morrison replied that the concept of reincarnation was a part of early African-American tradition. She felt that Beloved's reincarnation was appropriate to the book's time period—and once again she pointed to white reviewers' failure to understand African-American ideas.

Many African-American scholars and authors were angry at the white community's reception of *Beloved*. When the book failed to win either the National Book Award or the National Book Critics Circle Award, two important national prizes for writers, many felt that Morrison had been snubbed. In January of 1988, 48 African-American writers signed their names to a letter of protest that was published in *The New York Times Book Review*.

Morrison may have been disappointed that *Beloved* did not receive either of these two prestigious awards, but she was pleased that so many black Americans had joined together to voice their support of her work. She believed strongly that African-Americans needed to strengthen their sense of community—and she saw the letter as a sign that they were doing just that.

A few months later, in April of 1988, Morrison was selected to receive the most prestigious writing award of all, the Pulitzer Prize. Some thought the award had been made to soothe the anger expressed in the letter published in *The New York Times*, but most agreed that *Beloved* deserved the prize. Morrison insisted that winning the Pulitzer Prize proved nothing. She was flattered, but the award did not change her life in any way. She refused to let all the attention go to her head. Instead, she returned her attention to writing. The completed *Beloved*, she felt, told only a third of the story she wanted to tell. She had two more books to write.

A Busy Year

Toni Morrison's next book, *Jazz*, the second in the trilogy that *Beloved* began, is set in Harlem in the 1920s. Inspired by her parents' stories about their youth, Morrison wanted to show how ordinary people had lived in that period of history. She used jazz music as the book's central metaphor because, she told *The Chicago Tribune*, jazz "symbolizes an incredible kind of improvisation, a freedom in which a great deal of risk is involved."

The book tells the story of Joe Trace, a middle-aged door-to-door salesman who has two women in his life: Violet, his wife, and Dorcas, his 18-year-old lover. This love triangle, and the tragic conclusion that the story avows from the outset, serves as the story's center, the medium Morrison uses to explore her characters' sorrows and secrets. *Jazz* opens: "He fell for an eighteen-year-old girl with one of those deepdown, spooky loves that made him feel so sad and happy he shot her just to keep the feeling going."

Morrison developed the book's plotline while she was looking at *The Harlem Book of the Dead*, a book of photographs taken of dead loved ones. One of the pictures in this book showed an 18-year-old girl lying in a coffin. According to the text, on the night of the girl's death, while dancing at a party, she suddenly slumped to the floor. Those around her saw that she was bleeding, but when they questioned her she replied that she would explain on the following day. Later, her friends and family discovered that she had been shot by her jealous boyfriend. If this girl had sought help, her life might have been saved; but she wanted to protect the man she still loved. By refusing to implicate him, she gave him the chance to escape capture.

In *Jazz*, Joe Trace has killed his 18-year-old lover. The rest of the story explores his motivations. Morrison uses a series of flashbacks to explain each character's point of view, and the reader comes to understand that Joe, Violet, and Dorcas all have lost someone important. Joe's parents abandoned him in his youth, Violet's mother committed suicide because she was exhausted by her poverty, and Dorcas lost her parents to riots.

For all the tragedy in the story, however, the book holds a note of hope; ultimately, *Jazz* is about not death but survival. Morrison shows the healing that Joe and Violet undergo as they begin to put their lives back together after Dorcas's death.

Although the word "jazz" is never used anywhere except in the book's title, music is an important thread running through the Harlem neighborhood in which the story takes place. Even more, Morrison's language itself reflects the rhythms and harmonies of music. According to one reviewer, "You do not read this book; you listen to it."

Some critics said once again that Morrison's writing went too far; they felt her language was exaggerated and contrived, that it got in the way of her story. Most reviewers, however, praised the book, and it was soon on the *New York Times* bestseller list.

Morrison had another book on the bestseller list in that year as well. In 1992, she also wrote a book of literary nonfiction, *Playing in the Dark: Whiteness and the Literary Imagination*. The book's three essays had originally been presented as a series of lectures at Harvard University in 1990. The essays examined the racial attitudes of early American authors, including Edgar Allan Poe, Mark Twain, Ernest Hemingway, and Willa Cather. Until now, Morrison asserted, literary critics had always ignored the role of race in their critiques of early American literature. Her essays demonstrated that race had been a very real subtopic in many American writings. This often affected the author's work positively, but the debt the work owed to African-American culture had never before been acknowledged. Morrison showed that white writers had been inspired by the lives and language of black Americans. For instance, she told *The Chicago Tribune*, "black characters were used to represent endless love, like Jim in *Huckleberry Finn*."

Not only did Morrison write a novel and a book of criticism in that year, but she also edited and contributed to another book of essays. This book, *Race-ing Justice, En-Gendering Power*, was a response to the controversy between Anita Hill and Clarence Thomas.

In October of 1991, Clarence Thomas was nominated to the Supreme Court. Anita Hill, a professor of law at the University of Oklahoma, challenged Thomas's appointment on the grounds that he had sexually harassed her in the past. Thomas denied her charges, and in the end the U.S. Senate confirmed Thomas's appointment to the Supreme Court. The hearings left many questions unanswered, though. The United States began to look at sexual harassment in a new way.

Morrison believed that Clarence Thomas had tried to erase his "blackness" in order to become more acceptable to the American public. Anita Hill's accusations were intolerable because they "re-raced" him, and thus she became the guilty one. Morrison felt that America needed a formal response to the hearings. *Race-ing Justice, En-Gendering Power* was a collection of essays written by various academics in response to the questions that were still being asked nationally. Morrison wrote the introduction, "Friday on the Potomac." The title of her essay linked the Senate's hearings on an October Friday in 1991 with Daniel Defoe's *Robinson Crusoe* and his man Friday. In Defoe's book, the man Friday has to learn his master's language—but in the process he loses his own tongue, along with his identity; Clarence Thomas, Morrison claimed, was in the same sad predicament. Her book of essays was published in the fall of 1992.

But as busy as she was with her book projects, Morrison continued to find time for teaching, now at Princeton University, and for lecturing. Since her sons were grown by now, she had more free time than she had had in the days when she was a busy mother raising them by herself.

Her older son, Ford, was a flautist, a guitar player, and a sound engineer; he had followed in the musical footsteps of Morrison's mother, Ramah Willis Wofford. Morrison's younger son, Slade, had taken after his father. He was a budding architect and had just earned a degree. As a gift, Morrison had given him a year abroad, something she herself had longed for in her youth.

Financially, Morrison had come a long way from her childhood; she now owned two homes—one near Lake Carnegie and the other on the Hudson River—and was paid $10,000 for a single lecture. In fact, some of her academic colleagues were jealous of her wealth and prestige. Others resented the fact that she refused to participate in Princeton social life.

As usual, however, Morrison was very clear about her priorities. She knew if she was to accomplish all she wanted, she could spare no time. Some felt that for her to teach undergraduates was also a waste of her time and talents, like "asking a Rolls Royce mechanic to work on a Fiat," but Morrison didn't mind making time for teaching. She believed that teaching, like writing, is a powerful way to shape the imagination of others—and while she challenged her students, she too was challenged. She told the magazine *Lear's* that her students impressed her immensely; they "fly, absolutely fly."

Princeton, where she now taught, had once been an all-white university, a school for rich boys who arrived on campus with their black servants. The atmosphere at Princeton had been changing, however, under the leadership of Harold Shapiro, Princeton's first Jewish president. Shapiro had recruited a group of African-American professors, and Morrison had become the group's leader. Together, this group of scholars was working to redefine the role of African-Americans within American history.

Morrison was delighted to be a part of this group. She had set a task for herself: to make Americans realize the "dark, abiding Afro-American presence" that had been on the periphery of the nation since its inception. She wanted to change the way in which America imagined itself.

Her personal fame and the popularity of her books now made her one of most prominent voices of the African-American community. But her greatest distinction still lay ahead.

A GREAT HONOR

On October 7, 1993, Morrison began her day as usual: she awoke at 4:30 in the morning to write. She had been working peacefully for a few hours when the phone rang. The sound of the phone made her heart sink; she was convinced that if someone was calling her so early in the morning it must be bad news.

When she picked up the phone, a friend's voice said, "Did you hear?" Morrison's sense of dread was overwhelming. She was certain now that something awful had happened. But she was wrong. Her friend was calling to congratulate her: Morrison was to be awarded the 1993 Nobel Prize for Literature. She would be the eleventh American to win a Nobel Prize, the eighth woman to be chosen for an award in literature, and the first African-American. In its citation, the Swedish Academy, which administers the honor, praised Morrison for the "visionary force and poetic import" of her six novels. It went on to speak of the "epic power" of her fiction, with its "unerring ear for dialogue and richly expressive depictions of black America."

The news swept across the Princeton campus, and reporters gathered to interview Morrison. But when she arrived on campus, the reporters were told they would have to wait. Morrison had to teach her literature class before she could talk to them. For her, it was business as usual, no matter what had happened.

In fact, she could hardly believe that the news true; she kept thinking it must just be a rumor. Finally, later that day, she received an official phone call from the secretary of the Swedish Academy, confirming that she was indeed the winner. A letter was on its way. "Why don't you send me a fax?" Morrison asked. She felt that if she had a paper in her hands she would know that the whole thing wasn't a dream.

It wasn't a dream. Speaking through her publisher, Knopf, Morrison formally expressed her gratitude for the prize. "I am outrageously happy. But what is most wonderful for me, personally, is to know that the prize at last has been awarded to an African-American. Winning as an American is very special—but winning as a black American is a knockout."

Although she was in the process of writing a new book, now she had to lay her writing aside to travel to Stockholm, where she would receive the award. There was much to be done. First, she had to write an acceptance speech. She had little free time in which to work on it, though, and when she stole some time to devote herself to the speech, she still could think of nothing that satisfied her. Moreover, she had to find something to wear, which was nearly as hard a task as writing the speech. "I called someone at the Nobel Committee," she joked to *Time*, "and I said, 'Look, if you're going to keep giving prizes to women—and I hope you do—you're going to have to give us more warning. Men can rent tuxedos. I have to get shoes, I have to get a dress.'"

The flood of congratulations and invitations to other events made it even harder for her to find the time to prepare. Finally, though, she put together a speech—and designer Bill Blass, a friend, came to her rescue with a dress. He took her to his fitting rooms and had her groomed for her appearance at the awards ceremony. For Morrison, the experience was unreal. "They had everything," she told *Time*; "they had all these people around trying to make something work on me. On me." Little Chloe Wofford had certainly come a long way.

Two months later, she traveled to Stockholm, where she spent a busy week attending various events, including concerts, dinners, and press conferences. At last, after lunch at the American Embassy, she was driven with a police escort to the Swedish Academy, where she was to give her Nobel lecture.

The short, gray-haired woman, dressed to the floor in black sequins, stood up and said, "Once upon a time...." Using the words that generations of children have grown up hearing, she slowly told the story of a woman who was born both blind and wise. The audience of 400 people listened attentively, reading from the copies of her speech that they held in their hands. The only sound in the hall was Morrison's rhythmic voice and the rustle of paper when the listeners turned their pages. When she finished, the audience rose to their feet in a standing ovation.

The actual presentation of the award came three nights later. The festivities began with a trumpet fanfare, and the king of Sweden escorted Morrison at the head of the procession. Morrison's sister, her two nieces, and her two sons all were there that night to see her receive her award. And her mother, 87 years old and in a nursing home, was still alive to share her daughter's joy.

The prize's monetary value in that year was $825,000. When reporters later asked Morrison what she would do with the money, she had no answer. "This is new to me," she told them, "having to decide what to do with money. I have no history of making such decisions."

Morrison hoped that her success would inspire younger African-Americans. She told *The New York Times Magazine*, "There were probably young people in South-Central Los Angeles or Selma who weren't quite sure that they could do it. But seeing me up there might encourage them to write one of those books I'm desperate to read. And *that* made me happy. It gave me license to strut."

Not everyone was happy that Morrison had won the prestigious award. Some critics compared her writing to that of other Nobel laureates, like John Steinbeck and Pearl S. Buck, whose preoccupation with social concerns—so the critics said—had dated their writing, leaving it no longer pertinent to the modern reader. Essayist Stanley Crouch concluded that Morrison was "immensely talented. I just think she needs a new subject matter, the world she lives in, not this world of endless black victims."

Morrison knew that some people believed she had won the Nobel Prize not because of her skill as a writer but because of who she was, an African-American woman. These suspicions were nothing new to her, though, and she shrugged them aside. "When I heard I'd won," she told *Time*, "you heard no 'Aw, shucks' from me. The prize didn't change my inner assessment of what I'm capable of doing, but I welcomed it as a public, representational affirmation of my work. I was surprised at how patriotic I felt, being the first native-born American winner since Steinbeck in 1962. I felt pride that a black and a woman had been recognized in such an international forum."

Ultimately, though, Morrison did not let the pride go to her head. Her personal priorities were still clear: she knew she had another book to write.

PARADISE

Toni Morrison's seventh novel, the third in the trilogy that *Beloved* had inaugurated, was entitled *Paradise* This book's first print run was an extreme 400,000 copies; the book was slotted to be a bestseller before it was even released.

After *Jazz*, Morrison had begun casting about in her mind for the central topic of her next book. Her constant reading eventually led her to a seldom-mentioned chapter in U.S. history: the westward emigration of emancipated slaves after the Civil War. These former slaves were lured by the promise of a new life in the open spaces of Oklahoma and other western territories. Morrison's imagination was engaged by a slogan she read in many of the newspaper advertisements for the western territories: "Come Prepared or Not at All." That strange and ominous phrase would eventually develop into a book.

The story of *Paradise* opens on a dewy Oklahoma morning in 1976 with a terse and brutal statement—"They shoot the white girl first." Then the novel flashes back through a century of history to explain who "they" are and why they are shooting the women who live in a decaying mansion. The roots of the brutal act are in the 1870s, when nine freed slaves with their wives and children head westward to settle in the Oklahoma Territory. After much hardship, they reach a town called Fairly, where they ask the local citizens for permission to settle; the inhabitants of the town are also African-Americans, but their skin is lighter than that of the new settlers. Ultimately, the settlers are rejected, an act that lives on in their memories as "the Disallowing."

"Afterwards," the narrative continues, "the people were no longer nine families and some more. They became a tight band of wayfarers bound by the enormity of what had happened to them. Their horror of whites was convulsive but abstract. They saved the clarity of their hatred for the men who had insulted them in ways too confounding for language."

The Disallowed families eventually establish a settlement of their own, Haven, where they live in isolation from the rest of the world. The town continues like this until World War II, from which the males return to find that the town is dying; the residents are moving out, looking for work in the cities. So the younger men decide to repeat their ancestors' history: they move their families further west to found a new community. They name this new settlement Ruby, in honor of a woman in the clan who died after the journey. Ruby is 90 miles from any other town, which is just what the men want; the land is described as "flat as a hoof, open as a baby's mouth." The only nearby inhabitants live in the Convent, a strange, old house 17 miles away.

A dying nun and her servant, Consolata, live at the Convent. Eventually, the Convent also becomes a sanctuary for runaway young women, women who need a refuge from their husbands, boyfriends, or parents. The two places—Ruby and the Convent—are like mirror images of each other, for in Ruby men rule, while women flee to the Convent to escape that rule.

The characters in *Paradise* all are mixtures of good and bad, even the proud, independent, and judgmental men. In the 1960s, the twins, Deacon and Steward Morgan, grandsons of one of Haven's founding fathers, are angry at the subversive attitude of Ruby's young people. They decide that something is polluting Ruby, and eventually they come to blame this deterioration on the influence of the women in the Convent.

Race is not often mentioned in *Paradise*. As readers get to know the women at the Convent, they do not even know which are white and which black, so they cannot guess who will be the first to be shot by the men of Ruby. "I did that on purpose," Morrison told *Time*. "I wanted the readers to wonder about the race of those girls until those readers understood that their race didn't matter. I want to dissuade people from reading literature in that way. Race is the least reliable information you can have about someone. It's real information, but it tells you next to nothing."

That Morrison should say such a thing is surprising, as she has spent her whole life speaking out on the issue of race. Still, she insists that in reality there is no contradiction between what she has written in the past and the position she takes in *Paradise*. Her life and work has always been a struggle against racial categorization; categories like these, she affirms, have always been used to disempower and to exclude groups of people.

The book's title raises questions in itself: What is Paradise? Can this perfect spot be found somewhere between the male-dominated Ruby and the female-dominated Convent? When an interviewer from *Time* posed the question to Morrison, she laughed. "It's not my place to define paradise for anyone. That, in one way, is what the new novel is saying. It's not anyone's place to do that."

But Morrison has her own ideas of what her personal paradise would be like. "Nine days of seclusion, total seclusion," she told *Time*. "No obligations, no demands, nothing but doing anything I wanted, when I wanted."

No Compromises

Each of Morrison's successes seems greater than the one before, but this does not imply that her life has been easy.

In 1993, the year in which she received the Nobel Prize, her brother George died; four other relatives died, too, in that same year. Her mother died shortly after she received the prize. And less than three weeks after her return from Sweden, on Christmas day, a fire destroyed her home on the Hudson River.

The fire was caused by a spark that escaped the fireplace and ignited a sofa. Morrison's son Slade was alone in the house when the fire started. He immediately called his mother, who was in Princeton, and she hurried to her home. One hundred firefighters from nearby communities arrived to fight the blaze, but they were unable to save the house. Several firefighters were injured, but no one in Morrison's family was harmed.

Many feared that valuable papers had been lost in the fire, but it turned out that Morrison had stored most of her manuscripts in her basement study, where they had escaped damage. For Morrison, however, the loss was immeasurable. She told *The New York Times Magazine*, "It isn't even about the *things*. It's about photographs, plants I nurtured for 20 years, about the view of the Hudson River, my children's report cards. . . ." Long ago, though, Morrison had learned an important lesson about survival; she knew that the ability to laugh could get her through any heartache.

And despite these losses, Toni Morrison's life continued to be busy and full. She still taught and wrote and lectured, and she also went on publicity tours for her books. Her popularity continued to grow.

In December of 1996, her third novel, *Song of Solomon*, was selected as the second offering of the Oprah Book Club. Morrison seldom watched television, so when someone told her the news, she was not impressed: who would want to buy a book, she thought, simply because Oprah Winfrey had recommended it? To her surprise, though, the effect of Winfrey's selection would be great indeed, far surpassing that of the Nobel Prize. Overnight, sales of *Song of Solomon* increased astronomically. The book eventually sold a million copies, and sales of Morrison's other books also jumped by 25 percent. Oprah Winfrey's purchasing the screen rights to *Beloved* even further augmented Morrison's notoriety and financial success.

Today, Morrison is wealthy. She has four residences: an apartment near Princeton University in New Jersey; another apartment in lower Manhattan; a stone house in Rockland County, New York; and the house on the Hudson River, which she has had rebuilt since the fire. When an interviewer from

Time asked her why she needed four homes, she shrugs and laughs. "I was a child of the Depression. I have bad dreams about eviction."

Morrison's family may have faced eviction and fire when she was a child, but today she has no reason to fear she will ever lack a place to live. She is grateful for the money—but she is not always comfortable with all the attention. She confesses that the publicity sometimes has made her irritable or depressed.

Morrison's deep commitment to the African-American community continues. Ironically, though, her fame and fortune have isolated her from the community in which she was raised. It is the ordinary people of that community about whom she writes—and yet she has become separated from them. The Toni Morrison of today has little in common with the populace of Lorain, Ohio; she can experience that community only through memory.

But she had little choice about leaving the town where she was raised. "If black people are going to succeed in this culture," she has admitted to *The New York Times Magazine*, "they must always leave. There's a terrible price to pay. . . . Once you leave home, the things that feed you are not available to you anymore, the *life* is not available to you anymore. And the American life, the *white* life—that's certainly not available to you. So you really have cut yourself off. Still, I can remember that world. I can savor it. I can write about it."

Morrison seems to be happiest in the rich world of her own imagination, but the emotional ties she has are strong ones, particularly her bond with her sons, to whom her commitment always has been a priority. Now that the boys are adults, Morrison lives alone; she has never remarried. She considered remarriage on several occasions, she has told *Time*, "[b]ut I decided against it for two reasons. I didn't want to give up the delight of not having to answer to another person, and I was worried about how my two sons would react to a stepfather."

Despite the busyness of her public life, her personal life is simple. She has a small group of friends, whom she sees occasionally—and she fills up the rest of her time with reading and gardening. "There have been mornings," she tells *Time*, "when I've gone into my greenhouse at sunrise, and the next time I checked it was noon." She is content to live in this intensely personal world.

Several times, Toni Morrison has predicted that she will not write more novels—and yet each time she completes a book, as the characters slowly loose their hold on her imagination, she begins to feel restless and lonely. She comes to miss the people who live so vividly in her imagination and whom she portrays so powerfully on paper. Eventually, a person or a phrase or event will begin to live inside her head, replacing the work she just finished, and around that one small detail another book will slowly grow.

And whatever she writes will continue to reflect the vast and mysterious world of the African-American imagination. She wants her writing always to demonstrate black Americans' combination of the supernatural with the details of ordinary life. As Morrison told an interviewer from *Contemporary Literature*, "We know that it does not bother [African-Americans] one bit to do something practical and have visions at the same time. So all the parts of living are on equal footing. Birds talk and butterflies cry, and it is not surprising or upsetting to them." Without a doubt, Morrison will continue to portray this view of reality with her unusual and lyrical choice of words and metaphors. This writing style, she insists, reflects the African-American oral tradition. It is part of what makes her books uniquely "black."

Over the years, Morrison has received countless awards and honorary degrees for her writing. But this recognition and the monetary success she has achieved were never the goal of her work. "There's a difference between writing for a living and writing for life," she told her creative writing students. "If you write for a living, you make enormous compromises, and you might not ever be able to uncompromise yourself. If you write for life, you'll work hard; you'll do it in a disciplined fashion; you'll do what's honest, not what pays."

Throughout her life, Morrison has always refused to compromise. "There were plenty of roadblocks along the way," she has told *Time*. "The world back then didn't expect much from a little black girl, but my father and mother certainly did."

Fueled by the confidence instilled in her by her parents, Toni Morrison has set for herself lofty goals. With the power and beauty of both her talent and her commitment, she has achieved them all.

THOMAS MARCH

Filling in the Gaps: The Fictional World of Toni Morrison

As Harold Bloom writes in his introduction to this series, "we can better find the work in the person, than we can discover that banal entity, the person in the work." That is, we can understand a writer's career as the public manifestation of an ongoing private dialogue, of the writer with her past and present writing selves. In the case of Toni Morrison, that dialogue reveals the engagement of a question that broadens as its contingencies and complexities reveal themselves in both the fiction and her other public writing.

In the evolution of Morrison's writerly persona, we can discern a connection between Morrison's fiction and her other public writing, political or otherwise. The non-fiction public writing stands not as a yardstick against which to measure the achievement of the fiction, but *with* the fiction, in a cohesion of purpose, an ongoing dialogue of expansion and refinement between the many manifestations of this particular writer's voice. In her novels—*The Bluest Eye* (1970), *Sula* (1973), *Song of Solomon* (1977), *Tar Baby* (1981), *Beloved* (1987), *Jazz* (1992), and *Paradise* (1998)—Morrison attempts to combat a false polarity, between docility and ferocity, that she claims has defined public consciousness of African-American life. She achieves this by creating a fictional world that enacts and describes etiologies of the full spectrum of African-American experience, of joy and pain, victory and defeat, and good, evil, and indifference, within communities of African-Americans themselves.

Morrison articulates this question in her responses to two events that become legible as stages upon which the nature of the social position of African-Americans is performed. In her introduction to *Race-ing Justice, En-*

Gendering Power (1992), a collection of essays on the confirmation hearings of Supreme Court Justice Clarence Thomas, Morrison writes, "Without individuation, without nonracial perception, black people, as a group, are used to signify the polar opposites of love and repulsion." In this text, as in her introduction to *Birth of a Nation'Hood* (1996), a collection of essays on the O.J. Simpson trial, she calls upon Melville's *Benito Cereno*, a narrative whose logic, she observes, requires a blackness condemned to reside at one of two impossible extremes—in a docility that evokes love or a primal violence that engenders repulsion.

It is this painfully false dichotomy between submissive docility and unpredictable ferocity, Morrison asserts, that persists in the representation and reception of African-Americans in the American consciousness.[1] It is one that, she suggests, cannot be comfortable even in its condescension—as in the supposed ease with which one can become the other (docility erupting into ferocity) this marriage of alternatives threatens chaos and requires an unwavering vigilance.

Morrison decries the notion of "race transcendence"[2] not only as an idea whose time has yet to come, but also as one whose invocation necessarily obliterates history and the struggles of definition and reconciliation that remain;[3] "the time for undiscriminating racial unity has passed,"[4] she claims, and differences in experience and perspective within the African-American community, as well points of intersection with other communities, can and must now be explored.[5] The world of Morrison's fiction is one that seeks to fill in the emotional and human history of African America in its own right—neither whitewashed nor separate, but a narrative that restores to the concept of "African-American" the full range of human experience.

The textual worlds that writers create may come into being as, in response to, or in celebration of attempts to negate the experience of a particular life. But from the great writer emerges an art-life, a life in the art, born, as Bloom suggests, of a struggle not only with tradition but with the writer's own past attempts to create this life, this textual world. This art-life establishes in its beauty and cohesion a truth that is self-sustaining, subject to its own laws, for better or for worse. Morrison's fiction does not sacrifice textual nuance to the exigencies of political or social testimony; to do so would make for dull and unconvincing writing, indeed, accessible only to those for whom the lessons of these particular struggles are already too real. The story of Morrison's novels to date is one of a writerly consciousness engaged in the elucidation of a question—one involving race, womanhood, and manhood—ultimately of *personality* and its complexities, of the contingencies of human experience and the consequences of reflection on that experience. Writ large, it is an attempt to understand and describe the peculiarity of the status of African-Americans as such. Writ small, it is nothing less than the question of who and how the individual becomes, in relation to a constellation of communities that inform the personalities of their members while simultaneously depending on them for their own existence.

After introducing *The Bluest Eye* with the slurred-together banalities of a Dick and Jane primer, Morrison allows her principal narrator, Claudia, to take over, with the simple superstitious explanation for the death of Pecola's baby, fathered by her own father: "there were no marigolds." The seeds they planted, the prayers they uttered, in a child's attempt to thwart evil by the commission of a good act, yield to a question: "There is really nothing more to say—except why. But since why is difficult to handle, one must take refuge in how." Here is the voice of a narrator who has come to realize the futility of innocent attempts to balance the injustice of the universe—to fathom and counteract the "why." One can only report, with the wisdom of the backward glance, the circumstances, the causes, surrounding an event that only she and her sister recognize as tragic—the death of an illegitimate child of incest, in itself symbolic of the casting-away that its desperately ugly mother has suffered throughout her life. Claudia testifies to how—through shame, disregard, and cruelty—Pecola comes to be. As Barbara Christian writes, in the context of what she sees as an emerging sense of belonging or of ownership of the community, as the novel closes, "Claudia. . . is able to wrest understanding rather than waste out of this new land."[6]

Morrison, already wary of the pitfalls of misunderstanding that arise from the availability of only one point of view, provides for the perspectives of even her most antagonistic characters. In her preface to *Deep Sightings and Rescue Missions* (1996), a volume of writing by Toni Cade Bambara, Morrison observes that, in contrast to Bambara's work, "[i]n some manuscripts traps are laid so the reader is sandbagged into focusing on the author's superior gifts or knowledge rather than the intimate, reader-personalized world fiction can summon."[7] Such "sandbagging," true, can be informative and interesting in and of itself, as a self-conscious demonstration of or meditation upon the nature of the writerly consciousness, or of the literary art in *all* consciousness—still, Morrison is on to something here.

It is this self-revelation, in the characters' own words and in the background that Morrison provides through narration, that allows the reader's judgment of each character to be tempered by understanding. Instead of leaving us wondering what could motivate Mrs. Breedlove to remain with an abusive husband, Morrison gives us the story of their early romance and courtship: she "needed Cholly's sins desperately. The lower he sank, the wilder and more irresponsible he became, the more splendid she and her task became." Just as Mrs. Breedlove has come to define herself in relation to Cholly Breedlove's misdeeds, Breedlove himself clings to his hatred of his wife as a way to maintain his own equilibrium: "No less did Cholly need her. . . . Hating her, he could leave himself intact." We have the story of Cholly's childhood, without a father, living with his Aunt Jimmy, who saved him when his mother tried to abandon him. His first sexual experience is interrupted by white hunters, who force him at gunpoint to continue for their amusement. As the hunters laugh, the origins of Cholly's hatred for his wife unfold: "Cholly, moving faster, looked at Darlene. He hated her. He almost wished he could do it—hard, long, and painfully, he hated her so much." Indeed, he may have survived the encounter with the hunters, but "it was Pauline, or rather marrying her, that did for him what the flashlight did not do. The constantness, varietylessness, the sheer weight of sameness drove him to despair and froze his imagination."

This understanding, however, is not intended to negate the severity of the implications, for Pecola, of the Breedlove's actions (or inaction). In this house, where hatred and self-definition go hand in hand, Pecola prays for her own invisibility, disintegration: "Please God. . . . Please make me disappear." Pecola's mother is a primary source, in addition to Shirley Temple milk mugs and the startling beauty of pretty girls like Maureen Peal, of the ideology of beauty that torments Pecola. She is also, however, its victim. To combat her own loneliness, Pauline Breedlove has become a chronic moviegoer, the effect of which has been her exposure to a standard of physical beauty to which her own family does not measure up. At the movies, "Along with the idea of romantic love, she was introduced to another—physical beauty. Probably the most destructive ideas in the history of human thought. Both originated in envy, thrived in insecurity, and ended in disillusion." Primed by the ecstasy of escape, Pauline absorbs the beauty she sees as beauty itself. The effect of this is not lost on Pecola, unaware though she may be of its origins. As the need to escape has led Pauline toward new ideas of beauty, the promise of beauty itself becomes Pecola's hope of salvation: "It had occurred to Pecola. . . if those eyes of hers were different, . . .beautiful, she herself would be different. . . . If she looked different, beautiful, maybe Cholly would be different, and Mrs. Breedlove too."

Pecola's eyes are the locus of her association of herself with this family—with ugliness of both presentation and circumstance. Pecola's form of belonging, to family and to community, is her obstacle. Claudia and Frieda have it relatively easy—Mr. Henry's sexual assault on Frieda is swiftly avenged. But Pecola is the stain that, as Pauline Breedlove does for Cholly, allows everyone else to feel better about her or his own situation. As Claudia later observes, "All of us—all who knew her—felt so wholesome after we cleaned ourselves on her." That Claudia, at least, has regretted this represents a promise of self-love and acceptance that might save a child like Pecola, but only by its universal adoption. Only a community unconvinced of its inferiority could free itself to love a Pecola. Claudia speaks for the possibility of such a community. It is Claudia who, rather than take on their assumptions of beauty as her own, destroys white dolls: "Dolls we could destroy, but we could not destroy the honey voices of parents and aunts, the obedience in the eyes of our peers, the slippery light in the eyes of our teachers when they encountered the Maureen Peals of the world." She hates Shirley Temple, while Pecola can't get enough of the milk that comes in a mug decorated with the star's cherubic face.

The only recourse for Pecola, in her desperation to acquire beauty and thus the attention of others that she has not only craved, but *needed*, is to leap from one pedophile to another. From the physical rape by her father, she flees innocently to a spiritual violation at the hand of Soaphead Church, the self-proclaimed mystic to whom she appeals for blue eyes. But he is only partially correct when he writes, in an angry, self-justifying letter to God: "No one else will see her blue eyes. But *she* will. And she will live happily ever after." Pecola's wish for eyes is granted by a reluctant prophet only when he sees the opportunity to use Pecola to get rid of his landlady's dog. It is an exchange of expedience, on both parts. And she does not live happily ever after; she gives birth to her father's child.

Pecola's dialogue with herself finally reveals her ambivalence toward her new blue eyes, mirroring the disillusion that Claudia, writing from the future, shares with regard to the circumstances that could have produced such a story as Pecola's. Returning to the fruitless planting of marigolds that inaugurated her story, Claudia informs us of "how I did *not* plant the seeds too deeply, how it was the fault of the earth, the land, of our town." Claudia's critique of the community in which she has been raised, and that abandons a girl like Pecola, is a reflection of Morrison's project. A relatively silent presence, Morrison allows her characters to reconcile their own accounts of events with their own histories, accounts of connection and disappointment whose circumstances spoiled the ground in which a girl like Pecola might otherwise flourish. It is in Claudia, in people like her, that hope for a more tolerant future resides: "More strongly that my fondness for Pecola, I felt a need for someone to want the black baby to live—just to counteract the universal love of white baby dolls."

The Bluest Eye is concerned primarily with the hatred *within*, the learned self-loathing of a community that is first thrust onto and then internalized by a particular girl. In *Sula*, Morrison continues to explore these themes of rejection and "otherness," but not directly as a matter of internalized racial self-loathing. "[T]he near-absence of whites in the novel," observes critic Maggie Galehouse of *Sula*, "forces a recognition of difference *within* race."[8] In spite of its centering on the relationship between two women as they grow apart, *Sula* is an account of a richer range of experience and community than we find in *The Bluest Eye*—accommodating, in the course of the stories of these two women, representations of community that range from motherhood, daughterhood, and friendship to guilt, defiance, and faith in reparation. In short, *Sula* explores the balance between asserting individuality and defying the community—and the modes in which the latter can be (mis)construed as betrayal.

The effect of Morrison's use of years as the titles of her chapters is to focus the reader's attention not only on the lingering effects of action, but also on the circumstances that, prior even to the characters' births, have contributed to their development. Ultimately, *Sula* is a novel about friendship, and its world comes into being in order to provide a space in which their histories may unfold in a way that enables us better to understand both these women as individuals and the social tensions signified by their unraveling relationship.

Sula Peace and Nel Wright, inseparable as they are, begin as very different girls and become very different women. Nel hails from a household in which her mother, Helene, demands order and propriety; Sula's household could not be more different. The most striking difference is that the Peace household accommodates a chaos unthinkable in Nel's home and emblematic of a more profound alienation from social convention, which Sula grows to embody. It is a house in which women reign, but it is a house in which female independence or assertion of self does not require a complementary demonization of the male. Morrison points out that, on the contrary, the self-sustaining Peace women embrace the presence of men: "It was manlove that Eva bequeathed to her daughters. Probably, people said, because there were no men in the house, no men to run it. But actually that was not true. The Peace women simply loved maleness, for its own sake." Although Morrison's use of the term "maleness" is perhaps too facile in this passage, she emphasizes, in the phrase "people said," the public scrutiny of private life and, more significant in this context, community assumptions about gender that will impede Sula's attempt to return to a life in Eva's house after years away. Moreover, Sula is introduced to an acceptability of sexual promiscuity at an early age: "Seeing her step so easily into the pantry and emerge looking precisely as she did when she entered, only happier, taught Sula that sex was pleasant and frequent, but otherwise remarkable." While establishing the special circumstances—in addition to race—that contribute to individual development, Morrison does not disavow the significance of racial identity;

rather, she expands the concept of identity to include race along with a range of other factors and influences. Of the troop of young boys she has taken into her home, Sula's grandmother Eva remarks, "What you need to tell them apart for? They's all Deweys." In spite of their differences in age and appearance, Eva calls them all by the same name; she groups them together as a concept. In doing this, she is mocking the racist's dismissive indifference to African-American individuality while at the same time underscoring the pervasiveness, even among those in the African-American community in which her family lives, of the impulse to reduce or to diminish the multifaceted nature of identity. It is an impulse that will ultimately destroy Sula.

Sula's comfort in these years, her friendship with Nel, is characterized from the beginning by a shared impulse to create a life free of those forces that define what girls *cannot* (or *may not*) grow up to be. Morrison describes this relationship both as having been founded on and as flourishing through connections of this kind: "Because each had discovered years before that they were neither white nor male, and that all freedom and triumph was forbidden to them, they had set about creating something else to be. Their meeting was fortunate, for it let them use each other to grow on." This description asserts the pair's dependence on each other for a shared identity. Indeed, we are told that, for Nel, "[t]alking to Sula had always been a conversation with herself." But self-definition is based on difference as much as, if not more than, on similarity, and the "growing on" that Morrison mentions foreshadows the girls' emergence into adulthood—achieved through self-definition by opposition.

Morrison remarks early in the novel, "Nel seemed stronger and more consistent than Sula, who could hardly be counted on to sustain any emotion for more than three minutes." But the difference between the two women, as it eventually manifests itself and broadens, is more complicated than a simple contrast betweens Nel's tendency toward repression and Sula's emotional unreliability. Nel assumes the roles of mother and wife. Sula's departure after Nel's wedding represents her acceptance, or at least awareness, of Nel's initiation into an adult world that cannot accommodate the closeness to which the two have become accustomed—or the commitment to self-definition that they once shared. As she remarks to Eva years later, on returning to her childhood home, "I don't want to make somebody else. I want to make myself." A friendship that begins as a shared defiance of the imposed consequences of difference in race and gender ends when only one of them remains committed to this defiance, and to such a degree, or for such reasons, that it destroys her.

Sula's tragedy is not an attempt by Morrison to argue against defiance and for conformity. Sula's rejections of community norms—in her sleeping with Nel's husband Jude, for example, or her committing Eva to a nursing home—represent not a resonance of the indifference to these standards that existed in the environment in which she was raised, but rather a reaction to her community's rejection of *her*. Armed with greater strength than a young girl like Pecola could have mustered, Sula nevertheless falls victim to the misreadings, conjectures, and resentments of a community that cannot accommodate her brand of self-assertion. In her status as the town's whore and devil, Sula further emerges as the necessary counterpart of Nel's—and the community's—position of righteousness. For some, the mark over Sula's eye might resemble a rose, but for others it represents "a copperhead," or the ashes of her mother, symbols that mark her as dangerous and cruel. The men despise her for having sex with white men. The mothers hide their children. Nel, after surprising Sula and Jude *flagrante delicto*, severs all ties until Sula is on her deathbed. Even her own grandmother reaches into the past to remember an evil Sula, one who watched motionless as her mother burned "not because she was paralyzed, but because she was interested." And although Sula eventually admits that she "stood there watching her burn and was thrilled," one is left to wonder to what degree this confession is influenced by Sula's weary, deathbed acquiescence in the town's mythology of her evilness. Her death leaves the town with no scapegoat, and the town turns against itself once again. The necessity of Sula-as-locus in the townspeople's mythos of their own righteousness is clear when Morrison writes that "[w]ithout her mockery, affection for others sank into flaccid disrepair." When the absence of Sula as a communal target of derision forces—or enables—them to regard each other more critically, it becomes clear that their unity and harmony have been false, too easy, obtained, as in *The Bluest Eye*, at another's expense.

Ironically, it is after Sula's death that the door to reconciliation finally swings open and the artificial nature of Sula's and Nel's opposition comes to light. The death of Chicken Little, a young boy teased by Nel and Sula, stands as a defining moment in their relationship, and its full importance is revealed to us only as Nel realizes her own culpability in the development of the self-destructiveness of Sula's opposition. After a visit to Eva following Sula's death, Nel recalls the moments after Chicken Little's accidental drowning, in which it was she, not Sula, who had demonstrated a steely, almost conspiratorial calm, in contrast to Sula's anxiety and guilt. She realizes that "[a]ll these years she had been secretly proud of her calm. . . .[and] [n]ow it seemed that what she had thought was maturity, serenity and compassion was only the tranquility that follows a joyful stimulation." It no longer matters whether Sula found her mother's burning terrible or fascinating, or both; the supposed aspirituality that such dispassion would imply is not Sula's alone but rather is shared by Nel. The binarism that has defined Nel's moral superiority to Sula breaks down, and Nel, although too late, seems to realize this herself. As she passes the cemetery in which Sula is buried, Nel laments both the loss of Sula and her own misconstructions: "All that time, all that time, I thought I was missing Jude." She has lost Sula by accepting, without question, the myth of Sula's nature that the community has propagated, by dealing with Sula's betrayal as the act of an unquestionably evil woman rather than as the venial straying of a friend with whom reconciliation will one day be possible. Her awakening comes too late, but that it comes at all is a merit one cannot ascribe to the town's other residents, who shun Sula even after her death.

Sula is ultimately defeated by her own cavalier defiance of life, which masquerades for years as an embracing. Sula's rejection of the possibility of approval begins with her mother's confession of disliking her. Reflexively rejecting the very idea of acceptance, instead of adopting the indifferent and truly independent posture of her mother and grandmother, leaves Sula accessible, not just sexually, to the unsympathetic imaginations of others. Reaction and defiance are the only tools of self-definition that she recognizes, and, as Morrison writes, "like any artist with no art form, she became dangerous"—not just in the consciousness of the community, but to herself. But lest we blame Sula for her inability to manage her mother's rejection in any way but a disbelief in the very possibility of acceptance, Morrison ultimately punishes the community that found it so easy to "wipe themselves" on Sula, as Claudia's community does on Pecola. In a fit of rage at being left out of the public-works project to build a tunnel under the river that runs by their town, the people of "the Bottom" conduct a spontaneous raid on the tunnel. Bent on destroying it, many of them lose their lives as the tunnel collapses around them. Phillip Novak observes of this novel, describing *Beloved* just as well, that "Morrison celebrates the precarious persistence of African-American culture by constructing a memorial to the losses that that culture has endured."[9] The tendency to jump to conclusions and act together out of spite or anger rather than engaging in productive—and direct—conflict may have enabled them to hasten Sula's wasting by withholding love and approval just as dramatically as she has rejected it, but it has led them to a destruction, by their own hand, that the racist whites of the neighboring towns could never have accomplished so effectively.

In *Song of Solomon*, Morrison extends her examination of the forces that both cement and challenge friendship, this time between two men, Milkman Dead and Guitar Bains. Milkman, like Sula, can only reconcile the contradictions of belonging and defiance by obliterating them through death. For Milkman, though, this is a choice, and one in which the annihilation of the self coincides with the realization of a fuller awareness of his history and of his relations to family and community.

Milkman's over-nurturing by his mother, encoded in this nickname he cannot shake, is balanced by the self-important under-nurturing of his father. Macon Dead is obsessed with improving his position and increasing his wealth; this requires of him not only a denial (both financial and emotional) of his sister and her family but also a denial of lingering questions surrounding his family history. It is only when a conflict arises between father and son that Macon is compelled to relate to Milkman more of his story. When Milkman is defiant about his father's prohibitions regarding his visits to his aunt Pilate, Macon responds with the story of his father and the farm, the story of his name, received from some drunken bureaucrat who had misunderstood his father's answers to his questions of origin and paternity. He ends this lesson by telling Milkman, "Let me tell you right now the one important thing you'll ever need to know: Own things. And let the things you own own other things. Then you'll own yourself and other people too." This advice, once taken, simultaneously initiates Milkman into his father's world of possessions and power and, ironically, alienates him from a more complete history of his family's origins and his own identity as a son. After Milkman strikes him in defense of his mother, Macon tells another self-serving story, of that mother's inappropriate love for her own father and how their intimacy always made Macon uncomfortable. Attempting to elicit sympathy, if not pity, from his son forces Macon to tip his hand yet again, revealing the roots of his blind ambition. At the root is an insecurity in his own power, represented here by his jealousy of his wife's filial loyalty: "I knew then they'd ganged up on me forever."

Milkman's adoption of his father's values comes at a price—it closes his eyes to his mother's suffering and to the precariousness of his father's apparent position of power. Macon has internalized a racial self-hatred that is not evident in the car, the money, or the property, for to associate these with "whiteness" is no better than to associate Pilate's world and its defiance of social norms with "blackness." The role of white oppression, and the nature of Macon's acquiescence to it, is apparent, rather, in the scene in which Macon arrives at the police station to pay Milkman's bail. Regardless of his own power and wealth, Macon adopts a posture of inferiority before the white policemen. While the necessity of this behavior clearly acknowledges the limits of African-American power as demarcated by white racism, Macon reveals in his behavior not that success is equated with whiteness, but that his success depends on the degree to which he can communicate a docility that allows him to maintain his position and his wealth, to divorce himself from the hint of threat, in either direction.

Indeed, Milkman's quest, although initiated by Macon for Macon's own purposes, becomes a quest to discredit the father and everything he stands for. The urge to discredit Macon is apparent in Milkman's confronting his mother during her visit to her father's grave. Rather than accept his father's assumption that these regular trips are visits to a lover, Milkman follows his mother to discover a truth that, while it supports some of Macon's suspicions, nevertheless undermines Macon's attempts to be the canonical source of family history by including the perspective of his mother. When Milkman finally accuses her of having nursed him too long, condemning him to bear this nickname, she unapologetically responds, "And I also prayed for you. Every single night and every single day. On my knees. Now you tell me. What harm did I do you on my knees?" Granted access to a more complete understanding of his mother's position and relationship with his father, Milkman is better equipped for the dismantling of Macon's mythology.

Milkman's friendship with Guitar provides him with an ongoing link to an alternative to his father's interpretations of the world. Guitar initiates Milkman into the history of the Dead family by taking him to see Pilate in the first place, whom Milkman previously "hated because he felt personally responsible for her ugliness, her poverty, her dirt, and her wine." The world of his aunt Pilate is one of unconditional love—a love, that is, whose only requirement is the family bond, not the acceptance of a particular version of the family history. Pilate debases herself for the sake of Milkman, having no other reason to do so than that she loves him and can. He's done nothing to earn the sacrifice of her dignity.

In Milkman and Guitar, we see a binarism of the kind that characterizes the relationship between Sula and Nel, but here this distinction is overt and articulated by the two friends in question. Milkman, acquiring competence in the world of his father's business, begins to find Guitar's world of politics and racial resentment distasteful. On the other hand, Guitar becomes less tolerant of what he views as Milkman's frivolity and lack of concern for the cause of African-American resistance of white superiority and the violence it engenders. When Guitar tells Milkman that he is "not a serious person," Milkman's only defense is that "[s]erious is just another word for miserable." Milkman's inability to contradict Guitar's assertion on more substantial grounds indicates that he is already beginning to distance himself from the wealth and power ethos of his father. Nevertheless, Milkman has not yet discovered a viable alternative, and he continues to resist the politics of racial vengeance that Guitar not only espouses but has committed to by joining the vigilante group the Days. Guitar explains his membership in the Days in terms of love: "What I'm doing ain't about hating white people. It's about loving us. About loving you. My whole life is love." Milkman's responds,

"Man, you're confused." Nowhere else in the novel are the inevitability and danger of confusion and misapprehension articulated as well as they are here, in Milkman's inability to reconcile the demands of the types of power and resistance exemplified by his father and Guitar. Milkman is right to reject Guitar's narrow understanding of what is at stake in the fostering of racial loyalty and unity, which Guitar describes: "Everybody wants the life of a black man. Everybody. White men want us dead or quiet—which is the same thing as dead. White women, same thing. They want us, you know, 'universal,' human, no 'race consciousness.' Tame, except in bed."

Milkman's quest for his father's gold and, finally, his family's true history, is a reconciliation of the most compelling forces in his life—his distaste for the narrow vehemence of Guitar's activism and his need to differentiate himself from his father—to define himself, once again, by opposition. Milkman's experiences in the land of his forefathers challenge the binary thinking that forces both father and son to disavow the experiences and perspectives of others in their community (or family), and to define themselves in terms at least as narrow as those by which *they* are defined. In Milkman's struggle, Morrison does not dismiss the notion of "race consciousness" itself in favor of some larger concept of identity that ignores race; rather, she suggests that this awareness involves an understanding of personal relationships that Guitar's ideas lack, despite his professions of feeling love. Guitar's love is abstract. Milkman comes to understand that a consciousness of oneself, of an identity that recognizes the importance of race *within* the context of personal relations, requires the reconstruction of the family history suppressed by Macon's rejection of any truth that might challenge his power.

What begins as a search for gold, the father's lost riches, ends as a quest for history, a filling in of the gaps left by personal memory, intended and otherwise. It is a filling in that transcends the father and denies Guitar's myopia, grounded in real outrage and love though it may be. Milkman fills in these gaps, recovering "Solomon" from the name of the town Shalimar ("pronounced *Shalleemone*"), recognizing Pilate's refrain of "Sugarman don't leave me here" in the song of the town's children "Solomon don't leave me here." He learns his grandparents' true names, and he comes to realize that the burden of bones carried by Pilate all these years is the body of her father. Returning to Shalimar with Pilate to bury the bones properly, in familiar ground, Milkman is forced to confront his conflict with Guitar once again. As Guitar shoots at him, convinced that Milkman has stolen the gold he promised to share, we realize that Guitar's single-mindedness has blinded him to the possibility that he has *not* been betrayed by his friend and, more important, to the significance of the task that Milkman has undertaken. The closing lines of the novel describe Milkman's final, suicidal confrontation with Guitar, in an attempt to end their conflict even if it cannot be reconciled: "As fleet and bright as a lodestar he wheeled toward Guitar and it did not matter which one of them would give up his ghost in the killing arms of his brother. For now he knew what Shalimar knew: If you surrendered to the air, you could *ride* it." Milkman's apparent suicide is an acknowledgement that he cannot defeat the dehumanizing unity of the Days but also that he has achieved a completion of sorts in having undone his father's denial of knowledge and resurrected the truth of his family's origins.

In *Song of Solomon*, Morrison again laments the human capacity for misunderstanding—Macon's of Ruth, Ruth's of Macon, Milkman's of everyone else, and everyone else's of him. Guitar's betrayal of Milkman emerges as the novel's most egregious misunderstanding, just as Milkman himself achieves a familial and cultural awareness that is alien to Guitar. The roots of Guitar's inability to comprehend Milkman's possible innocence or the project in which Milkman is engaged are present in Morrison's inauguration of the novel with Mr. Smith's suicidal leap. We learn only later that Mr. Smith's suicide is induced by the awesome responsibility of belonging to the Days, of sacrificing love for vengeance—of the human need for personal connection and touchable love, rather than an abstract love whose logic remains unsatisfying. In uncovering, and *re*covering, his history, Milkman has achieved a victory; he is no longer at the mercy of his father's repression of the family's origins, having replaced it with not only a fuller story of the last two generations of his family, but also with a family religion. In the context of her argument that Morrison refines the pastoral tradition to allow for an engagement of racial issues, Ann E. Imbrie writes that Milkman's transformation as the result of his experiences in Shalimar results in his becoming "at least sufficiently changed to understand and accept his human responsibilities."[10] The frozen core of the father's world begins to melt when Milkman, as a child, renews his access to Pilate's world. When he jumps from the cliff, in defiance of Guitar, it is consumed.

Tar Baby stands as a more direct assault on the tenacity of misunderstanding rooted in race—in the servant-master relationships in the "house" of the white American and in the souls of its African-American inhabitants. The household is full of misunderstandings. Valerian Street, retired candy mogul, has been ignoring the signs of wife Margaret's mental illness for years. He never sees his son, whose activist politics he neither comprehends nor respects. His two servants, husband and wife Sydney and Ondine, have served him for years, even before he retired to this island, Isle des Chevaliers, to escape his wife and Philadelphia society. That Sydney and Ondine's niece, Jadine, has been educated primarily at their employers' expense only increases their sense of obligation to Valerian. Early on, Margaret says to Valerian of Sydney and Ondine—summarizing, in fact, what are clearly Valerian's own assumptions about their status—"You couldn't pry them out of here. . . . They are yours for life."

However, it eventually becomes painfully clear, after the arrival of Son, an intruder whom Valerian welcomes into the home over the objections of everyone else, that kindness and solicitude do not negate or undo the real relations upon which the scenario in the Street house is founded. At a Christmas dinner to which Sydney and Ondine have been invited only as a last resort, Ondine finally expresses her resentment of the Streets. Ondine's self-assertion is met not only with hostility but with a disaffirmation of her perspective. Valerian makes his position quite clear when he announces: "I am being questioned by these people, as if, as if I *could* be called into question!" Racist slurs and self-acquittals flow too easily when this balance is challenged by outbursts against Margaret Street that imply their having been at the tip of the tongue all along, held in reserve for just such a moment.

Jadine finally turns to Son for comfort after this outburst, but from its inception the relationship is doomed by Jadine's social prejudices, which in turn are rooted in her compulsion to reject the significance of race for fear that it might consume her entire identity. Jadine's skepticism concerning the motivations behind any man's desire for her reflects her own confusion regarding the significance of racial identity. Reflecting on the desires of her former love interest Ryk, whom she has left behind in Paris, Jadine muses: "I wonder if the person he wants to marry is me or a black girl? And if it isn't me he wants, but any black girl who looks like me, talks and acts like me, what will happen when he finds out that I hate ear hoops . . . that sometimes I want to get out of my skin and be only the person inside—not American—not black—just me?" Jadine refuses to accept assumptions of how race should inform her identity, focusing instead on succeeding in the world. Comparing Jadine to Milkman in *Song of Solomon*, James Duvall observes that these are characters "whose subjectivities are split between a desire to assimilate to the values of the white middle class and the voices that urge them to acknowledge a black racial identity."[11] Her disavowal of the significance of race, however, prevents Jadine from acknowledging how the very struggle against those identities molds her and informs her behavior. She fails to honor and respect her only family and resists Son's love because of her discomfort with an idea of the "African-American" that she perceives as backward, without ambition—and as the only alternative to her closely guarded "race-free" identity.

Jadine's rejection of Son reflects her own discomfort with the implications of accepting race as a facet of her identity. Initially, Jadine demonstrates a need to characterize Son as a thug in order to reject him: "As long as he burrowed in his plate like an animal, grunting in monosyllables, but not daring to look up, she was without fear." A later memory reveals her reluctance to see her identity lost to a throng of indifferent suitors. But this initial route to comfort, through the characterization of Son-as-animal, is reflected even after they become lovers, in Jadine's attitude toward what she perceives as Son's lack of ambition and inappropriate nostalgia for his humble origins. Duvall observes that "[b]y taking Jadine to Eloe, Son hopes to reveal to Jadine an authentic African-American community, one that will cause her to abandon her investment in white culture."[12] But Jadine is just as wedded to her assumptions about what constitutes the value in life as Son appears to be to his. She chastises him aggressively: "Stop loving your ignorance—it isn't lovable." Jadine is frightened not of some primal, ferocious sexuality, but of Son's humanity, reflected in a comfort with his origins that, according to the way in which Jadine constructs her world, would require the abandonment of all other facets of self to the domination of a racial categorization.

The love between Son and Jadine is founded on escape—Son's from his past, Jadine's from a complicated web of obligations to family and benefactor from which she cannot free herself. Jadine and Son both reject each other and find each other irresistible. Each represents to the other a dimension of identity previously rejected out of fear; but rather than come to an understanding of these differences that will allow each of them to dismantle old prejudices, they work against each other, each attempting to remake the other in his/her own image. Son has sacrificed something, too, in defying Jadine's world: an idea of progress that transcends simply moving on from one's past.

"Each was pulling the other away," Morrison writes, "from the maw of hell—its very ridge top." After they move to New York, and during the trip to Eloe, it becomes clear that neither can be satisfied in the world of the other. After Jadine's departure, Son finds in her photographs a portrait of Eloe through her eyes, its dinginess, its lingering in a past that he wants to forget, a present to which he can't belong while loving Jadine, and a future that would entail the full sacrifice of that love. It is this awareness that enables him, finally, to escape the defensive cycle in which Jadine remains trapped and that has prevented their reconciliation.

Like *Song of Solomon*, *Tar Baby* ends with a choice. Thérèse, one of Valerian's former servants, leaves Son at the shore of the Isle des Chevaliers, having advised him with regard to Jadine: "Forget her. There is nothing in her parts for you. She has forgotten her ancient properties." It is the full range of her humanity that Jadine has forgotten, or that has been withheld from her because in the context of her own success, money and fame and life itself have required the sacrifice of the fundamental bonds of family and home, of reciprocal love in general—that characterizes the human. Ondine chastises, "A daughter is a woman that cares about where she come from and takes care of them that took care of her. . . . I don't want you to care about me for my sake. I want you to care about me for yours." And this is what is lost in the struggle to capitulate to the desires of a world of people who love her beauty for its exoticism, its hint of a rebellion possible with something to rebel *against*. But Son still searches for Jadine; finding her or not finding her is not the issue. Son's world has expanded to include the validity of Jadine's ambitions, and with its expansion comes new access to the world of myth and story of the island's original inhabitants. The journey that awaits him is the one he has avoided his entire life. It is one that will take him through the mythology of the past toward a greater understanding of the dynamics of his position that he can finally share with Jadine, should he be lucky enough to find her.

Beloved is, in many ways, Morrison's most ambitious attempt to fill in the gaps in the American understanding of the African-American experience, both in the range of the relationships it explores and in its examination of guilt, reparation, and the legacy of slavery. There is more to *Beloved* than an obvious argument about the evils of the slave system. Morrison's accomplishment is the creation of a world in which the dehumanizing conditions and lingering effects of slavery become emblematic of the struggle to reconcile the present with the past. Catherine Carr Lee notes of *Song of Solomon* that "through his initiation into the Southern community of his ancestors, Milkman gains. . . the understanding that the past continues to constitute the present in ways that are not constraining but liberating."[13] The struggle to achieve liberation in the face of a past whose accommodation is difficult to say the least is a theme to which Morrison returns in *Beloved*.

Sethe simultaneously represses memory and finds herself overwhelmed by it, and Morrison's narrative structure mirrors the coming into consciousness, fleetingly and incompletely, of Sethe's memory of murdering her daughter, Beloved. As if to balance the reality of the memory of murder that continues to emerge piecemeal, Morrison's narrator works with Sethe's own recollections to establish the abundantly nurturing aspect of Sethe's motherhood. Sethe, recalling her long trek through the wilderness toward freedom, remembers: "All I knew was I had to get my milk to my baby girl." When reunited with her children, Morrison relates, Sethe "kissed the backs of their necks, the tops of their heads and the centers of their palms. . . ."— swelling with love as with milk. Even after she has killed Beloved, she debases herself in order to pay for the engraving on the girl's tombstone of "the one word that mattered"—"Beloved." What is important is that she has loved the girl as she feels a mother should, sacrificing herself for the dignity of her child. That this love also motivated murder is a fact that does not lessen the quality of the love but, rather, reveals the extent to which the conditions of slavery pervert the most fundamental human emotions. The fact remains that, as much as she remembers, Sethe "worked hard to remember as close to nothing as was safe."

Paul D. represents an opportunity for Sethe to reclaim and accommodate the past and, in so doing, to proceed to a future in which pain may linger in memory but no longer excludes joy. Garner, the former proprietor of Sweet Home—the farm on which Sethe and Paul D. lived as slaves—had allowed his slaves to marry and to retain some pretense of their humanity; the crime is that this humanity was more than the conditions of their slavery would allow. It was predicated on Garner's continued power and on his need to nourish his self-concept as "tough enough and smart enough to make and call his own niggers men." Following Garner's death, a relative by marriage, known among the slaves as Schoolteacher, reduced their captivity to its essence, treating them like animals and forbidding the expressions of their human status that Garner allowed. Paul D. is unromantic about the time at Sweet Home, reminding Sethe that "[i]t wasn't sweet and it sure wasn't home." Sethe, however, responds that it was nevertheless the only kind of community they knew, at least before Schoolteacher destroyed it: "But it's where we were. . . . All together." On Paul D.'s arrival, Sethe begins to wonder whether his presence will bring with it a security that will allow her to confront the past: "Maybe this one time she could stop dead still in the middle of a cooking meal. . .and feel the hurt her back ought to. Trust things and remember things because the last of the Sweet Home men was there to catch her if she sank?" Paul D.'s return allows Sethe to remember but move beyond Schoolteacher's inhumanity, to integrate the pain of it.

But no future with Paul D. can be possible, no confrontation of or moving beyond the legacy of Sweet Home complete, until Sethe faces the consequences of having killed one of her daughters. Sethe's rationale is clear, and consistent with her claims of abundance with regard to her maternal nurturing; she killed the child, and attempted to kill the others, in order to protect them from a world in which the next Schoolteacher could deny their humanity. The domestic bliss that replaces the rancor of the baby ghost in Sethe's house reaches a pinnacle as Paul D., Sethe, and Denver return from the carnival. The image is of three people who love and support each other: ". . . [O]n the way home, although leading them now, the shadows of three people still held hands." The next line, however, which begins the next chapter, signals Beloved's arrival: "A fully dressed woman walked out of the water." Beloved arrives now because it is safe, not simply because she can enter into a world in which the conditions that led to her murder no longer exist, but because Sethe's repressive energy has been redirected toward the construction of a nurturing family. Beloved returns because it is safe to return, to a mother whose love can express itself in hand-holding, not in the slice of a saw across a neck.

However, Beloved's return is with demands for reparation. Seeking a forgiveness that Beloved cannot provide, Sethe's confrontation of this aspect of her past becomes an ongoing attempt at reparation that condemns Sethe to relive, rather than to reconcile herself to, the consequences of her actions. Beloved's demand is insatiable, and would kill Sethe were it not for the intervention of the women of the community, who gather at Sethe's home to pray for her and against Beloved. It is not their prayer but their presence that provides Sethe with an opportunity to recreate symbolically the scene of her earlier crime. Sethe, seeing Mr. Bodwin as a stand-in for Schoolteacher, attacks him with a knife. She has, in effect, re-enacted the scene of Beloved's murder, free now to express rage aggressively instead of protectively.

Beloved's departure after this reenactment suggests that she is satisfied that her mother's previous actions were motivated by love, rather than anger, by her inability to kill Schoolteacher and all that he represented, rather than a desire to kill her child. More important, Sethe can now reclaim her life, free from the guilt that has tied her to a past whose pain still breathes but whose logic no longer holds. That is, her struggle all along has been a matter of reconciling justifiable actions with a new reality in which they are no longer justified but their painful consequences still linger. As Paul D. says to Sethe, "we got more yesterday than anybody. We need some kind of tomorrow." While the pain is not something Sethe can erase, the only way to build a new life beyond, rather than *in*, that past is to assert her own humanity, in defiance of a world that sought to deny it and forced her, in order to keep them from living in that place, to attack her children.

In *Jazz*, Morrison returns to the theme of community misunderstanding, this time casting the world of the city as just as insular as the Eloe that Jadine despises in *Tar Baby*. But the biggest misunderstanding exists between Joe Trace and his wife, Violet. The larger community, the section of city that they call home, is simply a backdrop against which their own misunderstandings of each other can be reflected and shown in relief. The city mirrors the misapprehension and imperfect understanding that characterize the relationship. It also, however, provides the catalyst, in Dorcas, to their coming to terms with their mutual disappointment. In the novel's opening pages, the narrator opines, "[Y]ou have to be clever to figure out how to be welcoming and defensive at the same time. When to love something and when to quit." It is this struggle that defines the relationship between Joe and Violet Trace, as they find themselves growing older and confronting private disappointments and private pain that they must ultimately communicate to each other if they are to survive.

Their struggle reaches a climax in Joe's relationship with Dorcas and, moreover, the events that follow her murder. In a rage, Violet attacks the corpse as it lies in its casket; but Violet's anger stems not from mere shame or desire for revenge. She is torn between two concepts of Dorcas, as "the woman who took the man, or the daughter who fled her womb." Violet's mourning Dorcas' death, represented by her hanging a picture of the girl in their apartment, is fueled by both jealousy and regret, not so much that she has not provided Joe with a daughter, but that she has been unable to maintain the marriage. Indeed, it is a mother, not a daughter, that Joe has always sought. If nothing else, the story of Golden Gray and Wild, Joe's fugitive forest-dwelling mother, does explain why Joe would find himself tragically attracted to someone like Dorcas, so seemingly full of untamed youth. Her friend Felice describes that "[e]verything was like a picture show to her, and she was the one on the railroad track, or the one trapped in the sheik's tent when it caught on fire." Perhaps this is what Joe finds so irresistible: someone he can find and save, unlike his mother, and whom he can love without needing to struggle through the bitterness of loss, unlike his wife.

The Traces surface at the end of their agony to accommodate the presence of another young girl in their lives, Dorcas' friend Felice, indicating that they have reached a degree of security in their relationship that prevents the presence of a third party from representing a threat. Felice stands as a link to the memory of Dorcas that now stands as a warning to the Traces, but also as a surrogate daughter, someone whom they can love safely, untainted by any resentment they might have for each other. Observing the understanding that Joe and Violet finally achieve, however, underscores the depth of the misunderstanding and disappointment that have plagued their marriage since their arrival in the city. Joe and Violet have fallen into the trap of defending themselves against each other. As the Traces come to terms with the aftermath of Dorcas' murder, it becomes clear that welcoming betrayal, even one that disguises itself as compensation for a deep-rooted and painful loss, lays down a far too easy path from private resentment to public pain and loss.

In *Paradise*, Morrison once again examines the destructive nature of collective, compulsive misunderstanding that she explores in *Sula*. Here, however, an entire household of women falls victim to the unforgiving scrutiny and misdirected ire of the community they border. The Convent is situated several miles outside of Ruby, and thus the Convent women are "outsiders" by virtue of location as well as their having arrived, one by one, in flight from an assortment of pains and degradations inflicted upon them already by the outside world. *Sula* presents the story of one woman's defiance of the values and expectations of a downtrodden town. In *Paradise*, Morrison extends her argument to apply even to a thriving community, proud of its heritage and the purity of its composition, both racial and moral. Herein lies the strength of Morrison's argument, for if even a successful, thriving community can allow paranoia and self-righteousness to motivate injustice, then every community is susceptible. As Katrine Dalsgård notes, "a vast discrepancy has developed between the community's perfect and stable self-image and its actual conditions and cultural practices."[14]

The novel begins with the scene that will serve as the climax of the book: the town leaders' raiding of the Convent, a former mansion and Catholic mission that has become the repository of the town's sins. Referring to the motivations of the men, as she describes their ransacking of the Convent's rooms, Morrison writes: "That is why they are here in this Convent. To make sure it never happens again. That nothing inside or out rots the one all-black town worth the pain." The invasion of the Convent, which results in murder and the destruction of the community that these abandoned women have managed to fashion for themselves, reveals that the town has already become rotten, by the hubris and cruelty of the most prominent townspeople—specifically, Deacon and Steward Morgan, the town's twin patriarchs, of whom "neither one put up with what he couldn't control." The Convent is uncontrollable, its community of women harboring secrets about the town's powerful men that these men would never want revealed. More important, it is uncontrollable in its symbolizing past mistakes, of failure to make amends and repair the damage wrought by the appetites of the past.

The bulk of the novel explains the pain and shame that contribute to this climactic scene. Outsiders have come to *stay* outsiders, taking up residence at the Convent, presided over by Consolata. Once a castaway who was taken in by the nuns, she in turn takes in those who have nowhere else to go. Morrison tells us of the Convent's inhabitants that "[n]obody knew." And nobody *does* know, with any certainty, who they are, or how they spend their time. The novel tells not only the stories of these doomed women, but also what the people in the town do know of them: their generosity, their welcoming arms, their healing powers. These are women who have been abused, degraded, sometimes by the men of Ruby themselves. As Consolata explains to Mavis upon her arrival, lying is "not allowed in this place" but "every true thing is okay." This acceptance is precisely what leads to the Convent's downfall. Understanding is the primary rule of the Convent's community of cast-off women; accommodating, rather than judging and rejecting, the secrets and unmentionable desires of the townspeople has contributed to the town's associating this community itself with the impulses and urges whose origins they cannot acknowledge as residing within the town.

The voices that the midwife and mystic Lone hears as the men plot at the Oven, the community's meeting spot and a relic of the former town, provide both the rationale and, within that rationale, the underlying motivations for this attack. She overhears the mean explain: "They meddle. Drawing folks out there like flies to shit and everybody who goes near them is maimed somehow and the mess is seeping back into *our* homes, *our* families. We can't have it, you all." Indeed, "folks" go to the Convent in the first place *because* they are "maimed." The "mess" has always originated in their homes and seeks solace and release—*at* the Convent in times of need, and *in* the Convent when the memory of that need, its standing as a rebuke against their claims of perfection, becomes unbearable. Just as they and their wives, sisters, and friends have sought there comfort of various kinds, so do they seek one final comfort in the destruction of the place, which stands as a reminder that they have been weak.

Each of these tales, like the work of the writer in general, represents a search for understanding. In "The Dancing Mind," (1996) Morrison decries conditions that too often impede understanding: "The reader disabled by an absence of solitude; the writer imperiled by the absence of a hospitable community." She goes on to define "the life of the book world" as being "about making it possible for the entitled as well as the dispossessed to experience one's own mind dancing with another's." The purpose of such a dance, e.g. Morrison's novels, is to provide the reader, should the luxuries of solitude and receptiveness find him, with a fictional world in which to test and expand his concept of what the term "African-American" can mean. Morrison's novels urge us toward a unity beyond racial categories, one that fills in the gaps in the public consciousness of African-Americans while acknowledging the limits of understanding and connection.

It would be inaccurate to reduce Morrison's work to a discussion of simple equality or equivalence. It represents an expansion of the narrative space available for the African-American to occupy in the American consciousness. Morrison perhaps says it best herself, near the conclusion of *Playing in the Dark*: "My project is an effort to avert the critical gaze from the racial object to the racial subject; from the described and imagined to the describers and imaginers; from the serving to the served."[15] Over time, as the specific question of race evolves and even recedes, obliterated or replaced by a new set of exigencies that require newly unnatural creations of "natural" villains and monsters, the relevance of Morrison's texts, their intelligibility as near-history and too-near reality, will likewise evolve. What will remain is an examination of individuality and community, their mutually creative and destructive dance, that has been and will continue to be the essence of human experience.

Notes

1. Cf. *Race-ing*, xv; *Birth*, viii-xi.
2. *Race-ing* xxi.
3. *Race-ing*, xxviii-xxix
4. *Race-ing*, xxx
5. *Race-ing*, xxx
6. Christian, "Community and Nature: The Novels of Tony Morrison," *Black Feminist Criticism*, 49.
7. Morrison, *Deep Sightings*, viii
8. Galehouse, "'New World Woman": Tony Morrison's *Sula*," 339.
9. Novak, "'Circles and Circles of Sorrow': In the Wake of Morrison's *Sula*," 191.
10. Imbrie, "'What Shalimar Knew': Tony Morrison's *Song of Solomon* as a Pastoral Novel," 477
11. Duvall, "Descent in the 'House of Chloe': Race, Rape, and Identity in Tony Morrison's Tar Baby," 325.
12. Duvall, 339.
13. Carr Lee, "The South in Tony Morrison's *Song of Solomon* Initiation, Healing, and Home," 120.
14. Dalsgård, The One All-Black Town Worth the Pain: (African) American Exceptionalism, Historical Narration, and the Critique of Nationhood in Tony Morrison's Paradise," 233.
15. Morrison, *Playing*, 90.

CARL D. MALMGREN

Mixed Genres and the Logic of Slavery in Toni Morrison's Beloved

At first reading Toni Morrison's *Beloved* strikes one as an unusually hybridized text—part ghost story, part historical novel, part slave narrative, part love story. Indeed, some of its generic forms seem to rub against one another, to co-exist uneasily, in a state of tension, if not antagonism. The relation between ghost story and historical novel is a case in point. The conventions of the former involve the partial cancellation of the mimetic contract and demand from the reader willing suspension of disbelief in the supernatural. The historical novel, on the other hand, is based on a respect for the reality principle, for the world of historical fact; its basic allegiance is to the world as it is or as it has been. Morrison somehow holds these two disparate forms together. At the same time, Beloved can be seen both as a tragedy, involving a mother's moment of choice, and as a love story, exploring what it means to be be-loved. How do these forms fit in with the others? It might be argued that another narrative form, the slave narrative, holds the key to the narrative's unity. It is the institution of slavery that supplies the logic underwriting the novel, the thematic glue that unifies this multifaceted text.

In its opening sentences, *Beloved* announces part of its generic identity in no uncertain terms:

> 124 was spiteful. Full of baby's venom. The women in the house knew it and so did the children. For years each put up with the spite in his own way, but by 1873 Sethe and her daughter Denver were its only victims. The grandmother, Baby Suggs, was dead, and the sons, Howard and Buglar, had run away by the time they were thirteen years old—as soon as merely looking in the mirror shattered it (that was the signal for Buglar); as soon as two tiny handprints appeared in the cake (that was it for Howard). Neither boy waited to see more, another kettleful of chick peas smoking in a heap on the floor; soda crackers crumbled and strewn in a line next to the doorsill. Nor did they wait for one of the relief periods: the weeks, months even, when nothing was disturbed. No. Each one fled at once—the moment the house committed what was for him the one insult not to be borne or witnessed a second time. (3)

Beloved is clearly a ghost story, dealing with the "spiteful" or "sad" or "rebuked" spirit of a baby girl who died in a horrible way some years previously. The girl, Beloved, manifests herself initially as a poltergeist, haunting 124 Bluestone Road and those who have in some way betrayed her. Despite the fact that the spirit is a baby, she "throws a powerful spell" (4). But Paul D., the last of the Sweet Home men, exorcises this ghost soon after his arrival, and the restless and relentless spirit is forced to take more drastic means. She assumes a human shape, at the age she would have been had she lived, and returns to confront Sethe, the mother who has wronged her in two ways, first by murdering her, second by denying her. For eighteen years Sethe has been systematically "keeping the past at bay" (42), her days devoted to the "serious work of beating back the past" (73). The reincarnation of Beloved compels Sethe to confront her personal past, a past that up till then had been "unspeakable" (58), to come to terms with the fact that she murdered her baby daughter. In this novel, then, "nothing ever dies" (36), especially our private ghosts, the skeletons we think safely locked in our closets, at least until we put them to rest. Because "anything dead coming back to life hurts" (35), what Sethe must undergo is an agonizing private exorcism of her own.

Seen in this light, the novel takes on a supernatural character; it is a ghost story about one beleaguered woman's struggle with a real, but personal, demon. But Beloved is a novel that straddles generic forms, as the opening paragraph makes clear. It specifies that the novel's action takes place in the year 1873, at a house outside Cincinnati that "didn't have a number then, because Cincinnati didn't stretch that far," in a state, Ohio, that had been calling itself a state for only seventy years. The assignment of a number to an unnumbered house, the precision of the historical specifications, the reference to the passage of time, and the locus itself argue that this is a historical novel, obeying the conventions of literary historiography, among them an acceptance of the world of fact and a commitment to naturalistic interpretation. Beloved is very much situated in its historical time-frame; it makes reference to the persecution of the Cherokee Indians in the nineteenth century (111), to the history of Cincinnati (155), to the activities of the Ku Klux Klan in the 1870s, to the issues and incidents that engaged slaves and ex-slaves in the middle part of the last century—the Fugitive Bill, the Settlement Fee, manumission, Dred Scott, Sojourner Truth, the underground railway, the Colored Ladies of Delaware, Ohio. In chilling and graphic detail, the novel renders the experience of African-Americans before, during, and after the Civil War, in so doing enabling its readers to "experience American slavery as it was lived by those who were its objects of exchange" (Atwood 49). By fashioning a concretely particularized account of that historical experience, Morrison intends to make it come to life, to make it real, especially for those who, removed in historical time, "can't imagine it, despite the greatest good intentions and sympathy" (Schwartz B7). If Sethe must experience the "unspeakable" in her private arena, then we readers must experience the unimaginable in the public sphere.

It might be argued, however, that these two genres resist one another, that the concrete specificity of the historical dimension and its fidelity to the world of fact exert a kind of pressure on the supernatural dimension, encouraging readers to find a way to recuperate the text in naturalistic terms, to convert the text, in Todorov's terms, from the marvelous to the uncanny. The primary obstacle to this recuperation is, of course, the eponymous character Beloved, whose initial appearance in the novel is indeed miraculous—she is the "fully dressed woman" who "walked out of the water" (50). Can her existence and appearance be accounted for in realistic, non-supernatural terms? The evidence certifying her status as "real" ghost, as the precocious baby returned, is, after all, impressive.[1] She identifies herself immediately after her appearance as "Beloved," the name that Sethe had had inscribed upon the unnamed baby's tombstone. She asks Sethe about the "diamond" earrings Sethe used to wear, earrings that had been taken from Sethe during her imprisonment eighteen years earlier. Beloved has the skin and complexion of a newborn despite her eighteen years; her sole disfigurements—three parallel scratches on her forehead and a neck scar, "the little curved shadow of a smile in the kootchy-kootchy-coo place under her chin" (239)—would seem to be the stigmata left from Sethe's assault upon her. Finally, Beloved hums a song that Sethe herself made up and sang to her children, a song no one else could possibly know. Hearing the song, Sethe becomes convinced of "a miracle that is truly miraculous," the return of her baby girl (176).

Until that point, however, Sethe believes that there is a naturalistic explanation for Beloved's appearance: "she believed Beloved had been locked up by some whiteman for his own purposes, and never let out the door. That she must have escaped to a bridge or someplace and rinsed the rest out of her mind" (119). Morrison's dedication of the novel, to the "sixty million and more," points out a way of following up on this line of reasoning. The dedication honors, Morrison says, "the number of black Africans who never made it into slavery—those who died either as captives in Africa or on the slave ships" (cited in Otten 83). The dedication suggests the possibility that Beloved might herself be one of those unfortunates who experienced the slave ship passage, presumably smuggled in sometime before the Civil War and the establishment of the Northern blockade.

This hypothesis proves to be a powerful instrument of naturalistic recuperation. For one thing, Beloved's previously obscure, if not opaque, monologue (210–13) becomes accessible, if not transparent. The monologue reveals that Beloved is haunted by the slave ship experience; for her "it is always now there will never be a time when I am not crouching and watching others who are crouching too" (210). Troubling references within the monologue—to the crouching, the men without skin (the white slavetraders), the dead man on Beloved's face, the rats, the iron circle on her mother's neck, the noisy clouds of smoke (from the slavetraders' guns)—can all be fitted into the passage experience. This reading also explains Beloved's "unnatural" attachment to Sethe. The monologue specifies that the woman with Beloved's face (her mother) quite literally abandoned her daughter by throwing herself into the ocean:

> I cannot lose her again my dead man was in the way like the noisy clouds when he dies on my face I can see hers she is going to smile at me she is going to her sharp earrings are gone the men without skin are making loud noises they push my own man through they do not push the woman with my face through she goes in they do not push her she goes in the little hill is gone she was going to smile at me she was going to (212)

Beloved's mother goes in of her own accord; she chooses death before slavery (at about the same time Sethe is making a very different decision when confronted with very similar circumstances). Having been abandoned by her original mother, Beloved attaches herself to the reincarnation of that mother (Sethe) like a parasite.

Other references in the text fill in the rest of Beloved's history, confirming Sethe's original speculations about the girl. Beloved herself admits that she knew one white man (119). Presumably, he had kept her hidden and locked up her entire life, including a period of eight years after the end of the Civil War, using her for truly unspeakable purposes. This possibility is validated by a rumor Stamp Paid relates to Paul D.: "Was a girl locked up in the house with a whiteman over by Deer Creek. Found him dead last summer and the girl gone. Maybe that's her. Folks said he had her in there since she was a pup" (235). The fact that the white man called her "beloved in the dark and bitch in the light" explains the name she chooses for herself. Other mysterious circumstances—the earrings, the scars, the song—can be accounted for by not-improbable incidents drawn from her personal history or from her close association with Denver in the days following her arrival at 124. In some such way, one can fully naturalize Beloved's existence, appearance, and behavior. Beloved is in this reading the ultimate victim of slavery, a living reminder of the brutality of the institution.[2]

And yet, the novel Beloved insists throughout that it is indeed a ghost story, that it must be read in those terms. The poltergeist haunting 124 is undeniably real, giving tangible proof of its existence: it turns over slop-jars, causes sideboards to move, projects a paralyzing pool of redlight, assaults Here Boy the dog, and envelops the house in a cacophony of voices. Elsewhere, Morrison has insisted upon the place of the supernatural in her work; she tries, she says, to blend

> the acceptance of the supernatural and a profound rootedness in the real world at the same time with neither taking precedence over the other. It is indicative of the cosmology, the way in which Black people look at the world. We are a very practical people, very down-to-earth, even shrewd people. But within that practicality we also accepted what I suppose could be called superstition and magic, which is another way of knowing things. . . . That kind of knowledge has a very strong place in my work. (Morrison, "Rootedness" 342)

Within the narrative ontology of the novel, one must acknowledge and accept the existence of ghosts. Beloved in fact represents an example of Todorov's fantastic, a narrative form inviting and validating both natural and supernatural readings of its preternatural phenomena.

Beloved is thus both ghost story and historical novel. Indeed, at the thematic level, Morrison finally makes the one form reinforce the other, linking them through her reconception of the institution of slavery. If, as part of the supernatural dimension of the novel, Sethe must come to terms with a very real ghost from her personal past, something that forces her to deal with the atrocity she committed in that past, then too, within the historical dimension, we readers must come to terms with our own ghost, the spectre of a ruthless and dehumanizing institution whose legacy we have yet to acknowledge fully. In historical terms, slavery is a very real ghost from our collective past, one that we must confront personally if we are to exorcise it. The novel suggest that in some form "the slave past lives on, raising havoc" (Snitow 25). By personifying slavery as history's ghost, Morrison reimagines the institution and its legacy as a kind of abnormal excess that finally defies rational explanation, a ghastly figure from out of a nightmare. Indeed, she gives the novel the name of a character who is the ultimate historical victim of slavery, someone totally brutalized and dehumanized, someone reduced to a ghost of herself. And, the coda to the novel tells us, Beloved's story is so horrific, so much a bad dream, that within the black community it is deliberately repressed: "it was not a story to pass on" because in a case like this "remembering seemed unwise" (274). The black community can choose to forget Beloved, as perhaps America has chosen to forget the legacy of slavery, but for readers of the novel it is not that simple; they hold in their hands the very document that rehearses for them the story of slavery and its aftermath, thus memorializing Beloved's suffering and incarnating history's ghost. In this way, the novel serves as a form of incantation, the ritualistic calling forth of the spirits of the past.

If Beloved is both a ghost story and a historical novel, it can also be characterized as a love story, exploring what it means to "be-loved." In various places the novel propounds a spectrum of possible relations between lover and loved one, between Self and Other. The hard-headed Ella tells Sethe, "If anybody was to ask me I'd say, 'Don't love nothing'" (92). For Paul D. the only safe alternative for slaves and ex-slaves is to "love small" (162): "The best thing, he knew, was to love just a little bit; everything, just a little bit, so that when they broke its back, or shoved it in a croaker sack, well, maybe you'd have a little love left over for the next one" (45). When Sethe confesses to Paul D. what love made her try to do to her children, the shocked Paul D. can only tell her that her kind of love is "too thick," to which she retorts, "Too thick? . . . Love is or it aint. Thin love aint love at all" (164).

The novel thus meditates upon and mediates between the various forms that love takes. In this regard, its dominant theme is the problematics of love, particularly as regards the question of identity. The key love relation in this particular historical context is the maternal one; the novel consistently foregrounds the relation of mother and child and the dangers and delights of mother love. Morrison has admitted elsewhere an interest in this relation: "One of the nice things that women do is nurture and love something other than themselves—they do that rather nicely. Instinctively, perhaps, but they are taught to do it, socialized to do it, or genetically predisposed to do it—whatever it is, it's something the majority of women feel strongly about. But mother love is also a killer" (cited in Rothstein C17). The novel examines in what circumstances mother love can be a "killer" (cf. *Beloved* 132). Can we relate this thematic framework, this discourse on maternal love, to the logic informing the novel's multigeneric identity?

Central to the issue of maternal love, at the ethical heart of the novel itself, is the tragic action that Sethe takes against her children, her loved ones, an action that she feels was "right because it came from true love" (251). How finally do we judge this action? Morrison herself has been forthcoming but deliberately ambiguous about this aspect of the novel: "It was absolutely the right thing to do," she tells an interviewer, "but she [Sethe] had no right to do it" (cited in Rothstein C17). This sort of categorical and logical illogic is echoed in Sethe's own justification: "if I hadn't killed her she would have died and that is something I could not bear to happen to her" (200).

The normative dimension of the novel thus hinges upon our assessment of Sethe's action, about which there is certainly no critical consensus. Martha Bayles blasts the novel, just because it excuses Sethe from "lasting blame": "a slave commits a crime, but it is not really a crime because it was committed by a slave. The system, and not the slave, stands unjustly condemned for a deed that would possess another meaning if committed in freedom" (40). In a similar vein, Stanley Crouch argues that the novel tends to exonerate Sethe: it "explains black behavior in terms of social conditioning, as if listing atrocities solves the mystery of human motive and behavior. It is designed to placate sentimental feminist ideology, and to make sure that the vision of black women as the most scorned and rebuked of victims doesn't weaken" (40). Terry Otten, on the other hand, says that the novel insists upon the "necessity of personal responsibility" (81), that Sethe's deed is finally "understandable but not excusable" (82). And Carol Iannone argues that the novel is finally ambiguous in its "treatment of the moral dimensions of Sethe's initial act of child murder" (63), and that this ambiguity is a function of a general authorial intention to "take no clear stand on the appalling actions she depicts" (61).

I would argue that the novel does indeed take a clear stand on the issue, and that the stand is itself a function of the logic underwriting the novel's multigeneric identity, the logic of slavery. In this regard, slavery—its logic and its legacy—serves as the figure in the novel's carpet, the cloth that links love story to ghost story and ghost story to historical novel.[3] In the former linkage, love story to ghost story, the key notion is "possession." Its connection to slavery and the historical dimension is rather straightforward, as shall be seen.

The novel's treatment of slavery makes clear that the institution perverts the relation between Self and Other, master and slave, by thoroughly dehumanizing both parties:

> Whitepeople believed that whatever the manners, under every dark skin was a jungle. Swift unnavigable waters, swinging screaming baboons, sleeping snakes, red gums ready for their sweet white blood. . . . But it wasn't the jungle blacks brought with them to this place from the other [livable] place. It was the jungle whitefolks planted in them. And it grew. It spread. In, through, and after life, it spread, until it invaded the whites who had made it. Touched them every one. Changed and altered them. Made them bloody, silly, worse than they wanted to be, so scared were they of the jungle they had made. The screaming baboon lived under their own white skin; the red gums were their own. (198–9)[4]

As Margaret Atwood has noted, slavery serves in the novel as a "paradigm of how most people behave when they are given absolute power over other people" (50). As the above passage graphically depicts, such power reduces people to animals, a truth brought chillingly home to Paul D. when he is forced to wear a bit in his mouth after an aborted escape attempt. Sethe's eyes are opened to the reality of her status at Sweet Home when she realizes that to schoolteacher she is nothing but a creature whose value is determined in an accounts ledger enumerating her human and animal characteristics.

Slaves as animals, slaves as objects, slaves as commodities—the common denominator here is the denial of the selfhood of the slave, the conversion of the Other to Object, the reduction of human beings to checkerpieces (23), counters, or commodities, This motif is figured most forcefully in Baby Suggs's personal history: in the way in which her seven children are taken from her only to disappear forever; in the fact that for most of her adult life she has no name but Jenny, the name on her bill of sale. When her owner finally asks her what she calls herself, her response is telling: "Nothing. . . . I don't call myself nothing" (142). Insofar as she is characterized by a "desolated center where that self that was no self [makes] its home" (140), she is indeed nothing. The novel makes it clear that this denial of humanity and selfhood takes place even under the more benign forms of slavery, such as Garner's, as Paul D. comes to realize: "Garner called and announced them men—but only on Sweet Home, and by his leave. Was he naming what he saw or creating what he did not? . . . Did a whiteman saying make it so? Suppose Garner woke up one morning and changed his mind? Took the word away" (220). In the master/slave relation, "definitions belong to the definer—not the defined" (190), and there can be for the latter no sense of self-definition. Such is the inexorable logic of slavery. In extreme circumstances, such logic leads from personal degradation to self-annihilation, from debasement to extinction. It is an awareness of this extremity that Sethe acts on when she tries to destroy her children: "That anybody white could take your whole self for anything that came to mind. Not just work, kill, or maim you, but dirty you. Dirty you so bad you couldn't like yourself no more. Dirty you so bad you forgot who you were and couldn't think it up. And though she and others lived through it and got over it, she could never let it happen to her own" (251). And, the novel says, if one contests or rejects the logic of slavery, as Sixo does, then one is quite literally reduced to nothing.

A sense of self is thus contingent upon personal freedom and autonomy. In this respect, Baby Suggs's son Halle, a slave all his life, is instinctively wise; he knows that there is nothing like freedom in this world, that it is the most precious gift he can give his mother. When Baby Suggs at last breathes the air of freedom, she looks at her hands and realizes that they belong to her; she becomes aware, for the first time, of the beating of her heart. In a very real sense she takes possession of herself; at the same time she assumes her rightful name. Sethe experiences a similar kind of ego formation immediately after her arrival at 124: "Bit by bit, at 124 and in the Clearing, along with the others, she had claimed herself. Freeing yourself was one thing; claiming ownership of that freed self was another" (95). Indeed, Sethe draws upon the agonies endured during her desperate escape attempt in order to construct and validate that selfhood, a selfhood she identifies with those she has suffered for, as she later tells Paul D.:

> I did it. I got us all out. Without Halle too. Up till then it was the only thing I ever did on my own. Decided. And it came off right, like it was supposed to. We was here. Each and every one of my babies and me too. I birthed them and I got them out and it wasn't no accident. I did that. I had help, of course, lots of that, but still it was me doing it, me saying Go on and Now. Me having to look out. Me using my own head. But it was more than that. It was a kind of selfishness I never knew nothing about before. It

felt good. Good and right. I was big, Paul D., and deep and wide and when I stretched out my arms all my children could get in between. I was that wide. (162)

Given the circumstances, Sethe's is a story of personal triumph, but her telling of it is troubling.[5] The frequent recurrence of forms of the first personal pronoun in the speech, for example, indicates the extent to which Sethe's identity is connected with this experience. This identification of her selfhood with the fates of her children, this "selfishness," determines Sethe's subsequent actions and informs our judgment of them.

For the fact is that Sethe so identifies her Self with the well-being of her children that she denies their existence as autonomous Others, in so doing unconsciously perpetuating the logic of slavery. In effect, both parties of critics are correct. The root cause of Sethe's action is indeed the institution of slavery, whose most terrible legacy is an awful logic of human relationship. The novel "drives home the meaning of slavery," one critic notes, by showing how, within Sethe, "the roles of master and slave, mother and child, have been fused" (Thurman 179). And yet, as Paul D. argues, Sethe's action was not only futile but also counterproductive; the novel acknowledges the awful power of slavery but finally holds Sethe responsible, insists that there had to be "some other way" (165). At one point Sethe says that she "wouldn't draw breath without her children" (203). It is this conflation of Self and Other that underwrites Sethe's justification of her actions: "The best thing she was, was her children. Whites might dirty her all right, but not her best thing, her beautiful magical best thing—the part of her that was clean" (251). The language Sethe uses here suggests that she has both appropriated and depersonalized her children. It is this aspect of Sethe's love that shocks Paul D., forcing him to condemn her: "This here Sethe talked about love like any other woman; talked about baby clothes like any other woman, but what she meant could cleave the bone. This here Sethe talked about safety with a hand-saw. This here new Sethe didn't know where the world stopped and she began" (164).

Not to know where the World stops and the Self begins—this is to deny the separate and inviolable existence of the Other. This kind of love has been infected by the logic of slavery, a logic that converts the Other into an object to be owned, into a possession. The idea of possession, of being possessed by that which we think we possess, thus serves as the unifying motif of the novel. This notion recurs throughout the monologues that emanate from 124 after the house has been converted to a world of its own, a hermetically sealed world in which all sense of the boundaries between Self and Other has been obliterated:

Beloved

You are my sister
You are my daughter
You are my face; you are me
I have found you again, you have come back to me
You are my Beloved
You are mine
You are mine
You are mine (216)

To be loved in such a way is to have being only in relationship, a state of affairs that readily metamorphoses into the idea of possession. The loved one, the beloved, is converted into a love object, a thing. To love in that way is truly to be possessed, to be haunted by a ghost. This kind of love is itself an abnormal excess, an unnatural spirit. As Baby Suggs wisely notes, "Everything depends on knowing how much, good is knowing when to stop" (87).

When Paul D. condemns Sethe, telling her in no uncertain terms that "what you did was wrong," he adds that there had to be "some other way" (165). Sethe denies the possibility of alternatives, but other episodes in the novel tend to undercut that blanket denial. The action of Beloved's mother on the slave ship represents one such alternative—suicide, the extinction of the Self. Sethe's own action at the end of the novel—attacking the master who would deny the Selfhood of the Other—represents another alternative. Indeed, it has been argued that it is just this action, Sethe's turning on the enslaver in order to save "her best thing," that serves to exorcise her personal ghost and enables her to get on with her life (Otten 94).

The alternative to "thick love," the kind of love that subsumes the identity of the Other, is the love that Sethe manifests for Paul D., love that respects the integrity and inviolability of the loved one. Sixo explains the kind of love he shares with Thirty-Mile Woman as follows: "She is a friend of my mind. She gather me, man. The pieces I am, she gather them and give them back to me in all the right order. It's good you know, when you got a woman who is a friend of your mind" (272-73). This kind of love befriends the Other, gathers up the fragmented pieces of the Other, restores the Other to itself. Only after Sethe has learned the limits of love, the reciprocity of love, only then do she and Paul D. have a future; only then can they look forward and not backward. The two of them, Paul D. says at the end of the novel, have had too much yesterday and not enough tomorrow. They have been haunted by yesterday's ghosts, the spectres of history and biography. They can only have a tomorrow when Sethe lays to rest the final ghost, the logic of slavery, and accepts that she alone is "her own best thing"—a proposition to which she can only respond tentatively, interrogatively: "Me? Me?" (273).

Notes

1. There are seven reviews of the novel reprinted in Contemporary Literary Criticism, Yearbook 1988 that deal directly or indirectly with the question of Beloved's identity. All seven assume that Beloved is indeed the reincarnation of Sethe's long-dead baby girl. Otten proposes a naturalistic explanation for Beloved's appearance (84), but does not go into detail about it. The reading I'm about to develop was first suggested to me by my colleague Inge Fink. I am grateful to her for her help on this project.
2. Morrison's own comments on the reality of the ghost are tantalizingly ambiguous: "I wanted that haunting not to be really a suggestion of being bedeviled by the past, but to have it be incarnate, to have it actually happen that a person enters your world who is in fact—you believe at any rate—the dead returned, and you get a second chance, a chance to do it right. Of course, you do it wrong again" (cited in Rothstein C17).
3. Pursuing this line of argument, one might note how Morrison is careful to weave together her disparate generic strands: at one point she links love story to ghost story by comparing motherlove to magic (4); at another she links slave narrative to ghost story by imputing to the white masters a kind of occult power (244).
4. Cf. Frederick Douglass's treatment of the relation between master and slave in Narrative of the Life of Frederick Douglass, An American Slave. chapter VII: "Slavery proved as injurious to [my mistress] as it did to me. When I went there, she was a pious, warm, and tender-hearted woman. There was no sorrow or suffering for which she had not a tear. She had bread for the hungry, clothes for the naked, and comfort for every mourner that came within her reach. Slavery soon proved its ability to divest her of these heavenly qualities. Under its influence, the tender heart became stone, and the lamblike disposition gave way to one of tigerlike fierceness." In its depiction of slavery, Morrison's novel is clearly indebted to this and other slave narratives.
5. Elsewhere Paul D. notes that more important than what Sethe had done is the claim she made about what she had done (164).

Works Cited

Atwood, Margaret. "Haunted by Their Nightmares." Rev. of *Beloved*. *New York Times Book Review*, 13 Sept. 1987: 1, 49–50.

Bayles, Martha. "Special Effects, Special Pleading." *New Criterion* 6, 5 (Jan. 1988): 34–40.

Crouch, Stanley. "Aunt Medea." Rev. of *Beloved*. *New Republic*, 19 Oct. 1987: 38–43.

Douglass, Frederick. *Narrative of the Life of Frederick Douglass, An American Slave*. 1845; rpt. Garden City, NY: Anchor, 1973.

Iannone, Carol. "Toni Morrison's Career." *Commentary* 84, 6 (Dec. 1987): 59–63.

Morrison, Toni. *Beloved*. New York: New American, 1987.

———. "Rootedness: The Ancestor as Foundation." In *Black Women Writers (1950–1980): A Critical Evaluation*. Ed. Mari Evans. New York: Anchor, 1984. 339–45.

Otten, Terry. *The Crime of Innocence in the Novels of Toni Morrison*. Columbia: University of Missouri P, 1989.

Rothstein, Mervyn. "Toni Morrison, in Her New Novel, Defends Women." *New York Times*, 26 Aug. 1987: C17.

Schwartz, Amy B. "*Beloved*: It's Not a Question of Who Suffered More." *Washington Post*, 3 Apr. 1988: B7.

Snitow, Ann. "Death Duties: Toni Morrison Looks Back in Sorrow." Rev. of *Beloved*. *VLS* 58 (Sept. 1987): 25–26.

Thurman, Judith. "A House Divided." Rev. of *Beloved*. *New Yorker*, 2 Nov. 1987: 175–80.

Todorov, Tzvetan. *The Fantastic*. Trans. Richard Howard. Cleveland: Case Western Reserve UP, 1973.

"Toni Morrison: *Beloved*: Survey of book reviews." *Contemporary Literary Criticism* 55 (1988): 194–213.

BARBARA CHRISTIAN

Community and Nature: The Novels of Toni Morrison

Between my completion of *Black Women Novelists* and its publication, Toni Morrison published a third novel, *Song of Solomon*. While her theme of the relationship between Nature and Community is certainly one important element in my previous analysis of *The Bluest Eye* and *Sula*, it seemed to me that Song of Solomon further refined this concern of hers. And since *Black Women Novelists* focused on the development of black women characters in the novels, I did not have the space to delve as much as I wanted into Morrison's philosophical orientation. "Community and Nature" focuses on this orientation while including an analysis of Morrison's most recent novel.

During the last eight years, Toni Morrison has created a world of her own in three critically acclaimed novels. Though different in emphasis, *The Bluest Eye* (1970), *Sula* (1974), and *Song of Solomon* (1977) present communities whose particular view of Nature transforms the air they breathe, the earth they walk. In few contemporary American novelists is the meaning of Nature so important as it is in the novels of this black woman writer. The interpretation of Nature is not only central to her characters' attempts to understand themselves, but to the fables Morrison weaves, the way she tells her tales.

Reprinted by permission of the publisher from Christian, B., *Black Feminist Criticism: Perspectives on Black Women Writers*, (New York: Teachers College Press, © 1980 by Teachers College, Columbia University. All Rights reserved.), pp. 47–63.

This particular theme of Morrison's, the relationship between her characters' belief system and their view of Nature, is basic to her works and is one of the principal reasons why her novels emanate a feeling of timelessness even as they are so pointedly concerned with the specificity of her characters' communities. The relationship between Nature and a particular human community is the kernel of the contemporary fable as Morrison has wrought it.

At first glance, each of her novels may seem to be primarily about one character: Pecola in *The Bluest Eye*, Sula in *Sula*, and Milkman Dead in *Song of Solomon*. But as we read the novels, what impresses us is not only these characters, but their blood relations. The people from whom the major characters derive their sense of themselves are as memorable, as finely drawn, as the focal characters. Who can read *Sula* without being struck by Eva, Sula's grandmother? As much time is spent in *The Bluest Eye* on Pauline Breedlove as on Pecola. And what would *Song of Solomon* be like without Pilate, Milkman's marvelous aunt? In fact, because Morrison penetrates the essence of her focal characters, we discover that a necessary aspect of their central conflict in the novel is their relationship to their natal communities, the people who gave them life. Like many oral storytellers, Morrison spins tales about how the characters' conduct of their lives is connected to their community's value system. Her novels present worlds that are very much like villages in which kinship ties are woven into the dreams, legends, the subconscious of the inhabitants.

That is why we are first introduced in these novels to the place that the characters inhabit, the land of the community. Like the ancestral African tradition, place is as important as the human actors, for the land is a participant in the maintenance of the folk tradition. It is one of the necessary constants through which the folk dramatize the meaning of life, as it is passed on from one generation to the next. Setting, then, is organic to the characters' view of themselves. And a change in place drastically alters the traditional values that give their life coherence.

Migration from the rural South to a more or less urban North has had great impact on the lives of Afro-Americans. And in the movement north, blacks not only migrated to large cities, as so much of Afro-American literature indicates, but to many small towns as well. The effect of such a migration on the characters of the novel is a major thematic consideration in *The Bluest Eye*. Morrison emphasizes the importance of this change by first introducing Lorain, Ohio as a land that would allow neither the marigolds nor Pecola to grow, even before we know the significance of the shriveled marigold seeds or who Pecola is. The characters we will focus on are recent arrivals to this town, whose connection to another place, the South, had been intense and life sustaining if only because they'd had to forge a tradition of survival against great odds. As new inhabitants, and as black people, they are looked down upon by the more established white community of Lorain, Ohio. The black migrants must therefore learn how to survive in this land that is at present a sterile one for them, even as they try to evolve a tradition that is functional in this place. Until they do, their lives will lack coherence.

Pauline, Pecola Breedlove's mother, is representative of the loss of a center with which these migrants are infected. Separated from the rural South, which allowed her privacy and freedom of imagination, and cut off from the tradition of her maternal ancestors, she falls prey to the destructive ideas of physical beauty and romantic love as measures of self-worth. Her life in urban Lorain, Ohio removes her from her customary avenues for expressing herself and for wresting some meaning out of her life. As a result, she lays the blame for her misfortunes on her incapacity as a black woman to be beautiful and therefore worthy of a good life. The difference between Pauline's adopted value system, derived from loneliness and the images of the movies, and the value system of southern black women, like her husband's Aunt Jimmy, is heightened in the novel. Lacking coherence in her own life, Pauline is unable to understand the effects of displacement on her husband and children. Women like Aunt Jimmy, however, had taken the limits of their existence and had transformed them by recreating them in their own image and in the image of their community. Both Pauline and Aunt Jimmy suffer, but their different perceptions of their self-worth are indications of the impact that a lack of functional traditions, as embodied in the land, has on a community.

Yet, even as we experience the tragedy of Pauline's daughter, Pecola, as a result of her feelings of total unworthiness that her family and her community have given her, we also begin to sense the stirrings of a viable tradition in this new land. For in spite of their obsession with Shirley Temple dolls and other golden symbols of the outer society's values, Mrs. McTeer and her circle of friends maintain their strong woman ties as well as an equally strong sense of family. As they absorb the different cycle of seasons that they now experience, they begin to see the town as their town, As a result, one of their daughters, Claudia, is able to tell us the story of Pecola Breedlove's tragedy and is able to wrest understanding rather than waste out of this new land.

In Morrison's second novel, *Sula*, she extends her introduction of the land beyond that of *The Bluest Eye*, for she tells us the story of the Bottom's beginnings. This tale is as much myth as it may be fact, for its core is the community's perceived sense of reality, its intuitive rendering of its precarious position in the hostile world. in presenting the Bottom's origins as a "nigger joke" and by juxtaposing its birth to its death, the author signals to the reader that her story will be concerned with the community's philosophy of survival. This philosophy, in Morrison's narrative, is very much related to the land—for the Bottom is actually topland where survival is precarious. But because a slavemaster, the previous owner of the land, had not wanted to pay his slave the good land he had promised him, he called this hilly land "the bottom of heaven." This black community is born, then, as a result of a white man's inversion of the truth, and it is destroyed years later when whites again alter the truth, the worth of the land, to suit their own desires.

Thus, a tradition evolves during the life span of the Bottom that is inextricably connected to its beginning, a tradition that is rooted in the nature of the land as the bottom on the top. Beset as it is by the hostile elements of heat and cold, wind and rain, the Bottom holds to the tenet that the only way one can defeat evil is by outlasting it. This view of resistance will be crucial to the story of Sula Peace; since she does not conform to the Bottom's view of woman, she is perceived by her community as a manifestation of the evil side of Nature. Rather than focusing its attentions on the pervasive evils of racism and poverty that continually threaten it, the community expends its energy on outlasting the evil Sula. Finally, the community's concept of resistance, which has its basis in its history and the vulnerability of the land, proves too weak in the face of the outside world to ensure the community's survival.

In addition to its vulnerability, the insularity of the land is a contributing factor to its distinctiveness Like *The Bluest Eye*, a change in place is crucial to the community, though for a different reason. The Bottom is so tucked away from the rest of the world that few of its women ever leave it. And when they do, they come back with a new perspective. Morrison emphasizes the impact of the exposure of these women to the outer world, as well as the infrequency of such occasions, by having Nel Wright leave her community but once. It is at this time that she learns she is an individual:

> "I'm me. I'm not their daughter. I'm not Nel. I'm me. Me." Each time she said the word *me* there was a gathering in her like power, like joy, like fear. (p. 24–25).

Such an appreciation of selfhood is contrary to the Bottom's definition of woman, as we discover when, years later, the marked woman Sula returns to the community after being absent for ten years. As *The Bluest Eye* focuses on the effect of a change in place on the community, particularly its women, so *Sula* emphasizes the effect of insularity on the women of the Bottom. As its conservative element, the women help the community retain its distinctive traditions. But because they are so insulated, the traditions of the community are seldom challenged and revitalized and are in danger of becoming obsolete. Thus, the nature of the land, its vulnerability, its insularity, its distinctiveness, will have untold effects on the black community in this novel and on the way major characters are perceived by that community.

Though distinctly different from her first two novels, Morrison's third novel is also characterized by her emphasis on the relationship between the nature of the land and the traditions of the community. Like *The Bluest Eye*, there are two black communities presented in *Song of Solomon*, one in the South and one in the North, which are contrasted though closely related. *Song of Solomon*, like Morrison's first two novels, begins with our introduction to one of these communities.

Significantly, the land that this community occupies is inseparable from that of the white community. Yet the newly arrived blacks retain some of their old traditions and transform the land through the process of naming, a process that keeps alive their own memories, their history as it develops. The importance of naming, of creating significance through the word, is a central theme in this novel. The black inhabitants of this town may not have any official power in the government of the town, but they hold their own as a community because they will not accept the names that others give to things that affect them. Thus, Mercy Hospital is named by the black community No Mercy, because they were not allowed there. By giving the hospital its correct name, they demonstrate the inversion of the truth that is operative in this land.

But, of course, the process of naming is also a tentative one. Because the community is controlled by others in areas critical to its survival, its names can also be changed. Like *Sula*, at the center of this novel's action is a "nigger joke" that has to do with naming. Just as the top is called the Bottom because of a white man's greed, so the Dead Family are erroneously named because of a white man's mistake. Nonetheless, this black family retains their dreaded name, for it paradoxically embodies their vitality as well as their oppression. And they perfect it by starting their own tradition of naming by randomly selecting the first names of their children out of the Bible.

Though many in the North would try to retain their collective memories through the process of naming the land, others would change their view of the land. In attempting to fulfill the promise that the North represents to them, these few would see it as an object for their use, for profit, rather than a hiving entity, an embodiment of their past. In their pursuit of money, they endanger the community by renting its fabric, by creating a hierarchy based on these who own things. The story of Milkman Dead is radically affected by the change in values from his southern grandfather's defense of his land with his life, to his northern father, who almost destroys his entire family in the pursuit of more and more property. And Milkman's search for gold, the profit from the land of his origins, which ironically he wants in order to free himself from his family, underscores the difference between the old traditions and the new. But the land reaffirms itself, for in his search for the gold, Milkman discovers a greater treasure, his real name and his roots in the land, which enable him to fly beyond it to a greater truth.

The land, then, on which the community dwells is not merely a place; it is one of the significant bases of its value system. And because Morrison sees human beings as part of the land, rather than apart from it, the community's view of Nature is crucial to the substance of her works. In all three novels, different societies' interpretations of Nature—as a physical or spiritual force, one that can or cannot be affected by human forces—are filtered through their definition of woman. The conflict between these different interpretations often results in the establishment of certain ideas of Truth by the dominant group—ideas that may, in fact, bean inversion of truth for other groups. Morrison's novels, thematically and structurally, are characterized by the use of inversion, sometimes in the form of humor, sometimes as tragedy, but always as a rendering of how complex any truth is. Like the blues, which fuses laughter and tears, her use of inversion portrays her villages as marvelously themselves even as they are infected by a different, usually hostile, world. Like Nature, her villages are both wonderful and terrible.

In *The Bluest Eye*, the central theme is the effect of the standardized western ideas of physical beauty and romantic love not only on the black women of Lorain, Ohio, but also on the black community's perception of its worth. All of the adults in the book, in varying degrees, are affected by their acceptance of the society's inversion of the natural order. For in internalizing the West's standards of beauty, the black community automatically disqualifies itself as the possessor of its own cultural standards. But beyond the statement of cultural mutilation that Pecola's desire for the bluest eye illustrates, Morrison challenges the unnaturalness of a belief system in which physical beauty is associated with virtue, and love is romance. Such a system creates a hierarchy in which only a few can be worthy of love and happiness, while the rest are condemned to yearn hopelessly for self-fulfillment. The thwarting of the natural urge for hove distorts the process of growth and rebirth of the land itself. Thus, the rape of Pecola by her own father in the spring, a dramatic instance of inversion, is related to the inability of the marigolds to sprout in the unyielding earth of the land: "The seeds shriveled and died; her baby too" (p.3).

The community's view of Nature as a disorderly process is also related to its acceptance of the paramount importance of physical beauty and romantic love. The struggle between the natural order, which involves funk and passion, and the desire for uncomplicated sweetness and light is embodied by the array of houses that Morrison presents. From the ugly storefront of the Breedloves to the standardized house of the Dick and Jane primer, the houses in this novel reflect the worth of their inhabitants according to the norms of the society and emphasize the destructiveness of a hierarchical order. Like the concept of physical beauty, the appearances of the houses, as measured by their inhabitants' ability or inability to erase the funk of nature, is an indication of their worth in the society. So that outward appearance rather than inner qualities becomes the measuring stick, and there must, by nature of a hierarchy, always be someone above and below each person who threatens her self-worth. As people come to believe that they *are* their appearance, they behave more and more as society expects them to. So the Breedloves fight and destroy each other in their ugly storefront because they come to believe in their own ugliness, their intrinsic unworthiness. The natural relationship they share as a family is distorted until the mother denies her own daughter for the white girl-doll who is her employer, the father finally rapes his own daughter in his search for godliness, and the daughter negates her own existence by pursuing and eventually obtaining the bluest eyes.

While the characters of *The Bluest Eye* are assaulted by the value system of another culture that has power over them, the characters in *Sula* are presented as having a world of their own. But though they may appear to be autonomous and separate, their continued survival is also gravely affected by the control of the outer society. In contrast to *The Bluest Eye*, the emphasis in *Sula* seems to be on the one quality the Bottom community shares with the world—their definition of woman, her span and space. In actuality, the impact of racism on their interpretation of Nature further reinforces this view.

The people of the Bottom do not believe that "Nature [is] ever askew—only inconvenient" (p. 78). Unlike the newly arrived inhabitants of Lorain, Ohio, they incorporate the funk and the sweetness, the evil and the good into their definition of Nature. But because Nature is so all encompassing, they use their feeling of human smallness as a bulwark against action and experiments. They relate their dictum, that Nature should be allowed to run its course, to the world of human events as well and therefore make no effort to alter them. But though the folk identify Nature and Evil as forces to be outlasted, they also believe that these phenomena express themselves through signs. Thus, the plague of robins or the mark over Sula's eye can be read if one has the wisdom to understand them. Not that this understanding can be used to alter the course of events, for these forces are perceived as indifferent ones that are slightly affected by human behavior. Rain falls alike on the good and the bad. And "the only way to avoid the hand of God is to get in it"(p. 56). As a result, the folk's only defense against evil is endurance. And in order to endure, they must hold tautly in place the commandment that woman must "make others." Their view of survival and of Nature exists only on the physical plane and is rooted in the fear of dying rather than in the desire to live. Convinced that they can only outlast the evils that are caused by humans, they do not pursue any other means of resistance.

Because of women's essential role in their struggle to survive, at least physically, the people of the Bottom might seem to be as slack in their toleration of female behavior as they are accepting in their attitude toward Nature. In the novel, they are willing to absorb the domineering style of Eva Peace, even unto her ritual killing of her only son in order to save his manhood; they avert their eyes from the free sexual behavior of Eva's daughter, Hannah; and they tolerate the hypocritical, high-toned behavior of the lady, Helen Wright. But in reality, they conform to a rigid bottom line—that the bearing of children or the relationship to males be central in a woman's life. That is why the friendship between Nel Wright and Sula Peace develops within these girls' recognition that because "they were neither white nor male, all freedom and triumph was forbidden to them" (p. 44). While Nel Wright eventually assumes her natural position according to the norm of the Bottom, Sula Peace insists on making herself.

Sula is similar to heroes, mostly male, in other American novels—the nameless narrator in *Invisible Man*, Damon Cross in Wright's *The Outsider*—in that she seeks her own individuality as a means to self-fulfillment. But as woman, her desire to make herself rather than others goes against the most basic principle of the community's struggle to survive. Since she does not fit the image of mother, the loose woman, or the lady-wife as Eva, Hannah, and Helene do, the community relegates her to their other category for woman, that of the witch, the evil conjure woman who is a part of the evil forces of Nature. In spite of their attitude toward Sula, the community does not expel her. Rather it uses heir, in spite of herself, for its own sake, as a pariah, as a means of reaffirming their oneness as a community. But in doing so, they block the creativity that is also a part of Nature—leaving it to seek destructive channels. Ironically, they achieve the opposite of what they intend, for they do not take from Sula what she has to offer them—the leap into living, the Insistence on knowing oneself, the urge to experiment and thus move forward. In allowing her to run her course, as they allow Nature to run its course, they surrender to death and destruction in the path of evil forces.

Morrison resists the idea that either individual pursuit or community conservatism is enough for fulfillment. Left without a context, the self has "no speck from which to grow" (p. 103), and deprived of creative spirits, the community succumbs to death and destruction. This Important though complicated idea is expressed in the novel through the author's exploration of the community's view that Sula is a selfish, unnatural woman and through the relationship of the community's well-being and eventual destruction of the River Road. Through much of the book, the men of the Bottom are excluded from helping to build this road because they are black. After Sula's death and a hard fall and a stingy Thanksgiving, many folk of the Bottom are drowned and suffocated when the tunnel for the road collapses. Exhausted from allowing Nature to run its course, exhausted from "hoping" that racism could be outlasted, the Bottom strikes an appropriate and tragic blow against the River Road they are not allowed to build and are physically destroyed. As Sula dies from self-absorption, so they die from their too-long insistence on mere survival. Later, after the road is built, the river subdued, white folks take over the now desirable land of the Bottom as it becomes what it was first called "the bottom of heaven."

Macon Dead, in *Song of Solomon*, would not have erred, as the characters in *Sula* did, on the side of letting Nature run its course. For his main goal in life is the acquisition of property as a means of securing more and more wealth. His view of Nature, representative of a rising middle class, is to own it, rather than to live within it. The importance of possession applies not only to Nature, but to his family as well. He possesses them and displays his wife and children as signs of his wealth. The result of this philosophical view of Nature and therefore of his family and his community is a movement away from life. In transforming the land into an object, into a thing that is not alive, he threatens to destroy the basis of his continuity, which is by nature, a part of Nature.

Just as Macon represents the ideology of a rising northern middle class, whose experience of racism in the South breeds in them an insatiable need for security, so Pilate, his sister, represents the tradition that identifies with Nature; it has no desire for material things. Pilate is presented in the novel as the healer of the spirit, the guide to essences beyond outward appearance or material things. Born without a navel, she learns how important, though misleading, appearances are to people. Thus, she learns to rely on inner qualities rather than outer manifestations. Yet paradoxically, her understanding of the spiritual is based on her appreciation of the land of her origins. Just as Macon's legacy is the land and the houses he owns, Pilate's "inheritance" is the bag of her father's bones. In some ways, this conjure woman without a navel who holds to no societal norms is very much like the marked Sula. But Pilate is able to do what Sula could not. She embodies the tradition of her family, of the southern community in which she originated, even as she makes herself.

The contrast in values between the Dead brother and sister is the axis of this third novel of Morrison's. The conflict between the Deads will attempt to resolve itself in the character Milkman Dead, Macon's son and Pilate's nephew. In a most significant way, Milkman is even more Pilate's child than he is Macon's, for without her conjuring, he would not have been conceived or born. Milkman must travel through the territory of his father's, the deadening effects of Macon's drive for money and security on his mother, his sisters and himself, as well as the geography of Pilate's, magic and its limitations. Milkman's quest for gold is propelled by his father's belief that Pilate's inheritance is gold rather than a bag of bones. And in the son's pursuit of the father's goal, he finds his grandfather's bones, the essence of the truth of his ancestors.

Milkman's process of discovering that truth is as complicated and as related to his community's view of Nature as the lesson that Nel Wright learns in acknowledging the relationship between Sula's life and death, and the life and death of the Bottom. For he finds that neither Macon nor Pilate's way holds the entire truth. One cannot fulfill one's self through the pursuit of wealth and security; nor can one live completely in the past.

In living apart from the world that now surrounds her, Pilate is not able to sustain Hagar, her granddaughter. "Not as strong as Pilate, not as simple as her mother Reba, Hagar could not make up her life as they had. She needed a chorus of women relations to give her "the strength life demanded of her—and the humor with which to live it" (p. 307). Unable to cope with the values of the world as it is, she succumbs to its terrors. The particular one that destroys her is interestingly enough linked to the major theme of *The Bluest Eye* and to the role that the community in *Sula* ascribes to woman. For in basing the whole reason for her existence on Milkman's love for her, Hagar comes to believe that he rejects her because she does not possess "silky hair," "lemon-colored skin," and "gray-blue eyes" (p. 316). Even the all-encompassing attention and love that she receives from her mother and grandmother cannot stop the poison of worthlessness that finally kills her.

Macon's way also results in death, as illustrated by the choked lives that his wife and daughters must endure. Seen primarily as symbols of his wealth and accomplishments these women are condemned to a life of ladyhood in which all passion is erased. As the daughter of the town's only black doctor, Ruth was bred to this narrow existence so thoroughly that all her passion is directed first to the father who gave her life, and then to the son whom she unnaturally nurses until late in childhood because she needs some physical contact, some connection with Nature. Her only outlets are the flowers that she grows and the watermark on the big table that connects her with the past. Ruth is symbolic of the terror that awaits those women who become the emblem of a man's wealth. Her son, Milkman, who also becomes an extension of his father's business, finds that at 35 he has no reason for being. It is only his inadvertent discovery of his grandfather's land and his great-grandfather's name that allows him to understand the reasons for both his father's and Pilate's point of view. And in understanding this ancestry, Milkman finds meaning in life, that he can fly beyond the preoccupation with earthy things.

The relationship between the community and its interpretation of Nature is not only a significant theme that runs throughout *The Bluest Eye*, *Sula*, and *Song of Solomon*; it is also one of the major structural elements of their composition. Based as they are on the interaction between her communities and Nature, Morrison's patterns are not just arbitrary, nor are they only a means of reinforcing her thematic emphasis. More importantly, her structural use of Nature is central to her rendering of her tales as fables, as stories that teach a lesson about life.

As in the fables of old, an interpretation of Nature is critical to the moral code of a particular human community. And implicit in the lesson is the awareness that although a particular interpretation of Nature might be assessed in a specific time, it refers to all time. In Morrison's novels, Time is a unified entity, rather than a chronology that is divided up into discrete fractions of past, present, and future, for it is the impact of significant events on the lives of the folk. In dramatizing the traditions of her community, Morrison's novels resemble the oral techniques of the storyteller, who tells her story in a particular time and in relation to a particular place, but whose treatment of Time and Nature endows the tale with those unbreakable connections between the folk of her community and the rest of the natural and human world.

In *The Bluest Eye*, the seasons, Nature's timing, are the major structural technique that Morrison uses to dramatize the unnatural inversion of truth contained in the ideas of physical beauty and romantic love. The book is divided into four sections, each named for the season in which an event is presented that has an overwhelming impact on Pecola as she enters womanhood. And we are prepared for their use in the structure of this novel by Claudia's introduction to the story: "Quiet as it's kept, there were no marigolds in the fall of 1941." Just as the mimicking Dick and Jane words that head each section remind us of the flat, standardized norms of the society, so the seasons reiterate the wonder and terror of Nature which is beyond standardization. As Nature's timing, the seasons also defy man-made systems of reckoning in which all is predictable, manageable, in which all funk is wiped away.

The language of the novel is based on this conflict between the natural order and the inversions of that order in human society. According to Nature, birds should fly and young things should grow, but they cannot, if their instinctive need for love and freedom is denied them. Morrison not only characterizes this conflict, she juxtaposes it to the perennial process through which human beings learn that in order to experience the preciousness of Nature and of life, they must also experience its meanness. This view of Nature is especially emphasized in the Winter section when the meanness of this season is disrupted by a false spring in the figure of Maureen Peal, the high-yellow dream child, whose physical appearance enchants everyone, but whose temperament is based on her knowledge that "she is cute," while the black girls like Pecola "are ugly, blackamoors." As trapped by her appearance as they are, she may not move beyond that assessment of her own worth. And though she is seen as the possessor of beauty, that most valued gift, she seeks knowledge about sex from Pecola with whom she identifies such things. Like Pecola, Maureen is assigned to an unnatural place in the order of human society. Her appearance, characterized as a false spring, is as much an inversion as is Pecola's name, associated as it is with the mulatta who hates her black mother in the movie *Imitation of Life*.

Throughout the novel, Nature, both constant and forever changing, is the basic metaphor through which Morrison's use of the inversion of the truth is sifted, so that the seasonal flow of birth, death, and rebirth is inverted in the human society. Pecola will not experience rebirth in the spring; rather she will be raped in the season of love by her father and will descend into madness in the sterile summer. Pecola will spend:

> her tendril, sap-green days, walking up and down, up and down, her head jerking to the beat of a drummer so distant only she could hear. Elbows bent, head on shoulders, she flailed her arms like a bird in an eternally grotesque futile effort to fly. (p. 162)

The use of Nature and Time as primary structural elements is perhaps even more pronounced in *Sula*. As in *The Bluest Eye*, the seasons naturally exert much influence on Morrison's community. But in *Sula*, the primal elements, rather than the seasons, are the aspect of Nature that is emphasized. And time is used in this novel more in terms of the folk's interpretation of it than as a part of Nature.

Sula is divided into a prologue, two parts, and an epilogue. The prologue introduces us to the Bottom, its birth and death, as based on the vulnerability and insularity of the land. Part I begins with another introduction, this time to Shadrack, the shell-shocked soldier who initiates National Suicide Day, a ritual that would get the fear of dying out of the way so "that the rest of the year would be safe and free" (p. 12). From this point on in the novel, we are shown those safe and free years, years that focus on Sula's and Nel's childhood, and then their experience as grown women in the Bottom. Finally, there is the epilogue called "1965," a year of understanding for Nel Wright, and a eulogy to the Bottom, a now extinct community.

What is initially striking about *Sula's* parts is that they are, in spite of Shadrack's ritual, permeated by death and are headed by the names of years. It appears that time is expressed in a chronological numerical fashion, but in actuality, it is not, for each year-chapter does not tell us what happened during that year, so much as it uses a pivotal event, usually a death that occurred in that year, as a point of focus for fusing the past, present, and future. Thus the chapter "1921" focuses on Eva's ritualistic burning to death of her son Plum in order to save his manhood. But most of the events related in this chapter do not occur in the year 1921; rather we learn about Eva's life and her personal qualities, qualities that will have considerable impact on her granddaughter Sula. Eva's sacrifices for her children, her domineering manner as well as her love of maleness are juxtaposed with her murder of her son and are absolutely necessary to an understanding of this most unnatural of acts. Time, in *Sula*, is not chronology but significant action.

This view of time is interwoven with fire, water, air, and earth in Morrison's dramatization of the relationship of the folk to Nature. The elements are the basic metaphor through which the chapter-years are presented. As a result, we come to see death as the most drastic consequence of the elements' interaction with human beings, often because of an inversion of the truth. Part I, for example, begins with chapter 20, Nel's journey to the funeral of the grandmother. That death is followed by Eva's ritual burning of Plum in the chapter "1921," which is connected to Hannah's accidental burning in the chapter "1923," both of which are separated by the accidental burning of Chicken Little by Sula and Nel in the chapter "1922."

The images of fire and water are particularly dominant in Part I. As both creative and destructive forces, fire and water have always been associated in the human mind with powerful spiritual forces and are symbolic of the inherent complexity of the natural order in which life and death are inextricably connected. These images, which are so prevalent in Part I, are fused in the chapter "1927," the last chapter of that section, when Nel marries Jude. This dream of a wedding, in effect, destroys Nel's sense of the individuality she had glimpsed in her one trip outside the Bottom and that had flourished in her friendship with Sula Peace. And we have been prepared for the symbolic reverberations of this wedding, which is Nel's initiation as a grown woman into the community. For as Eva, the dream expert, has told us in her analysis of Hannah's premonition of her own death, the dream of a wedding is death. This interpretation of a human ritual is consistent with the effects of the elements, for the wedding is seen as both death and birth. It is the end of Nel's enjoyment of her own individuality, the price she pays in order to take on the roles of mother and wife without which the community cannot survive.

The characters of this novel are also associated with particular elements. Eva and Hannah are associated with fire; Nel, Sula's best friend, is as consistent as the earth; Ajax, her lover, wants to fly. Sula, whose marked eyes are "as steady and clean as rain," (p. 45) is identified with water, that primal force which has power of fluidity but must be creatively contained within a form, or it will become destructive. It is the overflowing release of Sula's hurt emotions caused by her mother's words that she may love her but she does not like her that results in her accidental drowning of Chicken Little. And it is her fluidity, her need to explore and experiment that causes the community to turn her into a pariah. Because she has no context, however, her fluidity becomes destructive. Without a friend, she has "only her own mood and whim," and "Like any artist with no art form, she becomes dangerous" (p. 105).

The community, too, is associated with the elements. The people are "mightily preoccupied with earthly things," and the women are characterized as "bronze dusted with ash," their spirits rigidly contained within their bodies. Just as Sula crosses over into "a sleep of water always," the folk are destroyed by the excesses of the elements, as the earth turns cold then hot, and they are drowned or suffocated in the tunnel they were not allowed to build.

In *Sula*, the elements, particularly fire and water, are metaphors for the struggle that takes place between Sula and her community. In *Song of Solomon*, all of the elements are again used as structural points of reference, but this time the emphasis is very much on flying, on riding the air. Morrison uses the contrast between the artificial and natural to dramatize the two value systems represented by the Dead brother and sister. But beyond that conflict, Morrison uses the folk myth of the blacks in America who flew back to Africa, a myth that is found wherever Africans were enslaved, as the foundation of this work. In incorporating this myth into the story of Milkman's quest for gold, Morrison suggests that in order to be free, one must surrender to the most dangerous yet necessary of the elements—air. Air is the breath of life, and by learning to work with it, rather than trying to conquer it, one may learn to fly without even leaving the ground.

The first scene of the novel announces the centrality of this idea to the book, as well as the conflict between different value systems with which the black community in this midwestern town is confronted:

> The North Carolina Mutual Life Insurance agent promised to fly from Mercy to the other side of Lake Superior at 3:00. (p. 3)

In this introduction to the story of Milkman Dead, the mercenary philosophy of men like his father as well as the folk's connection with the still-living past, the artificiality of ladyhood as well as the naturalness of the desire to soar are all compressed into a scene much resembling a form of worship. Amid Mr. Smith's attempted flight in his blue silk wings, the artificial red velvet roses flying out of Ruth Dead's basket, and the singing of "O Sugarman done fly," Milkman begins his struggle down his mother's womb to be born. But as he enters the earth and grows older, lie learns that "only birds and airplane could fly." . . . "To have to live without that single gift saddened him and left his imagination so bereft that he appeared dull even to the women who did not hate his mother" (p. 9). The rest of this novel is concerned with Milkman's recapture of this desire and his final attainment of that gift. While Milkman is associated with flying, Guitar Bains, his best friend, is identified with the earth. A natural hunter, he misses the smells and sounds of the woods he had known in the South. He has the clarity of the earth. But like the earth, which is turned soggy by the blood of racism, he is maimed. He uses his natural capacity as a hunter to try to change the situation in which he and his people are caught, and his involvement with The Seven Days is his way of balancing the generations of blacks killed by whites. But in so doing, he must also snuff out his other natural instincts until he becomes totally absorbed with earthly solutions to the evils that surround him.

Song of Solomon is structurally based on the conflict between this preoccupation with earthly matters and the need to fly, that is by nature a part of each of us. The novel is divided into two parts. Part I emphasizes the tension between these two poles within Milkman's natal community in the North, while Part II traces the resolution of this tension as a result of Milkman's quest in his southern community. But in every section of this novel, these two thrusts are woven together, for there is continual interplay between the community of the North and the South, the past and the present, and Macon and Pilate's respective points of view. In developing the relationship of Milkman to these two communities, Morrison uses the elements as her structural guides.

Bereft of Nature's nourishment, Ruth Dead has but a few things that assure her that "the world was still there . . . that she was alive somewhere" (p. 11). One is the large watermark on her fine mahogany table, which connects her past to her present and "behaved as though it were itself a plant and flourished into a huge suede-gray flower that throbbed like fever and sighed like the shift of sand dunes" (p. 13). Another, for a time, is the nursing of her son beyond a reasonable age in the room that smells of damp greenness. This act is as much soaring as she is allowed and is the basis for her son's love-name. As Milkman's mother attempts to satisfy her need for nature in odd ways, his father staves off the fear, which he had acquired in his youth, of being a lonely, landless wanderer. By fondling the magic keys that declare him the owner of property he becomes landlocked. Pilate, on the other hand, is as landless as the birds. Though she would not set foot on an airplane, she is Milkman's pilot to another view of life. "A tall black tree," she is rooted in the earth even as she points to the sky.

In Part II, Milkman follows the trail Pilate had made in her youth. But instead of finding gold, that precious metal of the earth, Pilate's geography leads him to another community that is unknown to him, though a part of him. Again the elements are touchstones in his quest, for in Shalimar, the earth is not owned but lived with. The people are so much a part of it that they know the language that was before language, the language of the animals, of the earth itself. Milkman learns, through the music of the earth, the rivers, and the folk, the name of his ancestor, the one his father had glimpsed in his imagination years before:

> Surely, he thought, he and his sister had some ancestor, some lithe young man with onyx skin and legs as straight as cane stalks who had a name that was real. (p. 17)

Not only does Milkman find the onyx, the cane stalks, and the name, he discovers that this ancestor could fly. The knowledge of this legacy frees him and may help to free his family from the dead end that they are fast approaching, for one important ingredient in being able to fly is to know who you are.

But though Milkman now knows that the air can be a hospitable element, he must still suffer the consequences of his former quest for gold. The final scene of the novel is a climax of Morrison's use of the elements as structural basis. As Milkman and Pilate bury the bag of bones that is their inheritance, Pilate is shot by Guitar, Milkman's best friend, who believes that he has been cheated of the gold. And as Pilate dies, Milkman sings to her a song about their origins. Her death is followed, as if on the air of the song, by the appearance of a bird, which flies off with the earring box that contains her name. And from Soloman's Leap, the hand from which his ancestor flew, Milkman leaps into Guitar's arms, as he is transformed by the language of the rocks and the hills into a lodestar. In order to fly, he learns that he must surrender his life to the air rather than own it: "You want my life? You need it? Here" (p. 337).

The novel *Song of Solomon* is Toni Morrison's most recent exploration of the way in which the past myths of the folk and the significant events of their present merge to create still another variation in Nature's relationship to the human community. There is a consistency of vision in her three novels, for they all focus on the seemingly contradictory urges of human beings to be a part of Nature, yet distinct from it. Her characters instinctively yearn to be as fruitful as the earth, as fluid as water, as vivid as fire, as free as air. Yet they also live in human societies that are based on distinctions among their members. Morrison's dramatization of human societies emphasizes the tension between the natural order and the unnatural points of discrimination—race, sex, money, class—employed by human societies.

As a result, there is an admonition in these fables, which inevitably leads us back to the inherent desire for growth in each being, an admonition that this desire will manifest itself either in natural terms or in derangement. And because Nature is a part of each human being, it is too complex to be categorized or wiped away. Thus society's perennial attempts to ignore the relationship between human beings and Nature result in waste, pain, and often death.

Yet, as is true of most fables, Morrison's novels also remind us of the marvelous resiliency of Nature and therefore of human society—that though the marigolds may not sprout in the fall of 1941, they may in another year, if we understand the nature of the soil in which they shriveled; that water may be creative as well as destructive if it is allowed to discover a form that suits it; and that one may ride the air, if one is willing to surrender to it.

Notes

1. Toni Morrison, *The Bluest Eye*, Holt, Rinehart & Winston, New York, 1970.
2. Toni Morrison, *Sula*, Bantam Books, New York, 1973.
3. Toni Morrison, *Song of Solomon*, Alfred A. Knopf, New York, 1977.

Chronology

1931	February 18: Born Chloe Anthony Wofford in Lorain, Ohio, to Ramah and George Wofford.
1949	Graduates from high school and goes to Washington, D.C., to attend Howard University; joins the Howard University Players; adopts the name Toni.
1953	Receives a bachelor's degree in English with a minor in classics; goes to Cornell University in Ithaca, New York, for graduate studies in English literature.
1955	Receives a master's degree from Cornell; goes to Texas Southern University in Houston to teach English and humanities.
1957	Returns to Howard University to teach.
1958	Marries Harold Morrison, a Jamaican architect.
1961	Son Harold Ford is born.
1962	Joins a writers' group and writes a short story that will later become *The Bluest Eye*.
1964	Travels to Europe with her son and husband; is separated from husband; returns to Ohio, where son Slade Kevin is born.
1965	Accepts a position in Syracuse, New York, working for the textbook division of Random House; expands *The Bluest Eye*.
1968	Moves to New York City and becomes a senior editor for Random House, where she works with many African-American writers.

1970	*The Bluest Eye* is published.
1971–72	Teaches English at the State University of New York at Purchase.
1973	*Sula* is published.
1974	*The Black Book* is edited and published.
1976–78	Teaches at Yale University.
1977	*Song of Solomon* is published; Morrison wins the National Book Critics Circle Award.
1978	Named Distinguished Writer of 1978 by the American Academy of Arts and Letters.
1979	Moves to a boathouse on the Hudson River.
1980	Appointed by President Carter to the National Council on the Arts.
1981	*Tar Baby* is published; teaches at Bard College; is featured on the cover of *Newsweek*.
1984	Leaves publishing and accepts a professorship at the State University of New York at Albany.
1986	*Dreaming Emmett* is performed in honor of the first celebration of Martin Luther King Jr.'s birthday as a national holiday; the play wins the New York State Governor's Award.
1987	*Beloved* is published; Morrison lectures at the University of California at Berkeley.
1988	*Beloved* wins the Pulitzer Prize.
1989	Leaves the New York State University at Albany and accepts a position at Princeton University.
1992	*Jazz*, Morrison's sixth novel, is published, as is a book of essays, *Playing in the Dark: Whiteness and the Literary Imagination*; edits and contributes to another book of essays, *Race-ing Justice, En-Gendering Power: Essays on Anita Hill, Clarence Thomas, and the Construction of Social Reality*.
1993	Wins the Nobel Prize for Literature; her house on the Hudson Rivers burns; her mother dies.
1996	*Song of Solomon* becomes a selection of the Oprah Book Club.
1998	*Paradise* is published.

Works by Toni Morrison

The Bluest Eye, 1970.
Sula, 1974.
The Black Book, 1974 (conceived and edited).
Song of Solomon, 1977.
Tar Baby, 1981.
New Orleans (musical), 1983.
Dreaming Emmett (play), 1986.
Beloved, 1987.
Jazz, 1992.
Race-ing Justice, En-Gendering Power, 1992 (edited and contributed).
Honey and Rue (song cycle), 1993
Playing in the Dark: Whiteness and the Literary Imagination, 1992.
Paradise, 1998.

Works about Toni Morrison

Bell, Roseann, ed. *Sturdy Black Bridges*. Garden City, N.J.: Doubleday, 1979.

Bryant, Cedric Gael. "'Every goodbye ain't gone': The Semiotics of Death, Mourning, and Closural Practice in Toni Morrison's *Song of Solomon*," *MELUS* 24. 3 (Fall 1999): 97–110.

Butler-Evans, Elliott. *Race, Gender, and Desire: Narrative Strategies in the Fiction of Toni Cade Bambara, Toni Morrison, and Alice Walker*. Philadelphia: Temple University Press, 1989.

Carden, Mary Paniccia, "Models of Memory and Romance: The Dual Endings of Toni Morrison's *Beloved*," *Twentieth Century Literature* 45. 4 (Winter 1999): 401–427.

Chabot Davis, Kimberly, "'Postmodern Blackness': Toni Morrison's *Beloved* and the End of History," *Twentieth Century Literature* 44.2 (Summer 1998): 242–260.

Christian, Barbara. "Community and Nature: The Novels of Toni Morrison". *Black Feminist Criticism: Perspectives on Black Women Writers*. The Athene Series: An International Collection of Feminist Books. New York: Pergamon Press, 1985. 47–63.

Conner, Marc C., ed., *The Aesthetics of Toni Morrison: Speaking the Unspeakable*. University Press of Mississippi, 2000.

Dalsgård, Katrine. "The One All-Black Town Worth the Pain: (African) American Exceptionalism, Historical Narration, and the Critique of Nationhood in Toni Morrison's *Paradise*." *African-American Review* 35.2, 233–248.

Dubey, Madhu. "The Politics of Genre in *Beloved*," *Novel* 32.2 (Spring 1999): 187–206.

Duvall, John N. "Descent in the 'House of Chloe': Race, Rape, and Identity in Toni Morrison's *Tar Baby*." *Contemporary Literature* 38.2: 325–349.

———. *The Identifying Fiction of Toni Morrison: Modernist Authenticity and Postmodern Blackness*. New York: Palgrave, 2000.

Evans, Mari, ed. *Black Women Writers (1950–1980): A Critical Evaluation*. Garden City, NY: Anchor Press/Doubleday, 1984.

Galehouse, Maggie. "'New World Woman': Toni Morrison's *Sula*." *Papers on Language and Literature* 35.4 (Fall 1999): 339–362.

Grewal, Gurleen. *Circles of Sorrow, Lines of Struggle: Novels of Toni Morrison*. Southern Literary Studies. Baton Rouge: Louisiana State University Press, 2000.

Harris, Trudier. *Fiction & Folklore: The Novels of Toni Morrison*. Knoxville: University of Tennessee Press, 1991.

Heffernan, Teresa. "*Beloved* and the Problem of Mourning," *Studies in the Novel* 30.4 (Winter 1998): 558–573.

Holloway, Karla F., Demetrakopoulos, Stephanie. *New Dimensions of Spirituality: A Biracial & Bicultural Reading of the Novels of Toni Morrison*. Contributions in Women's Studies, No. 84. New York: Greenwood, 1987.

Imbrie, Ann E. "'What Shalimar Knew': Toni Morrison's *Song of Solomon* as a Pastoral Novel," *College English* 55.5 (September 1993): 473–490.

Jones, Bessie W. and Audrey Vinson. *The World of Toni Morrison: Explorations in Literary Criticism*. Dubuque, Iowa: Kendall Hunt, 1985.

Jones, Carolyn M. "Southern Landscape as Psychic Landscape in Toni Morrison's Fiction," *Studies in the Literary Imagination* 31.2 (Fall 1998): 37–48.

Kramer, Barbara. *Toni Morrison: Prize-Winning Author*. Springfield, N.J.: Enslow, 1996.

Lee, Catherine Carr. "The South in Toni Morrison's *Song of Solomon*: Initiation, Healing, and Home," *Studies in the Literary Imagination* 31.2 (Fall 1998): 109–123.

Lenz, Gunther, ed. *History and Tradition in Afro-American Culture*. Frankfurt: Campus, 1984.

Lesoinne, Véronique. "Answer Jazz's Call: Experiencing Toni Morrison's *Jazz*," *MELUS* 22.3 (Fall 1997): 151–166.

Malmgren, Carl D. "Mixed Genres and the Logic of Slavery in Toni Morrison's *Beloved*," *Critique* 36.2 (Winter 1995): 96–106.

———. "Texts, Primers, and Voices in Toni Morrison's *The Bluest Eye*," *Critique* 41.3 (Spring 2000): 251–262.

Mayberry, Katherine J. "The Problem of Narrative in Toni Morrison's *Jazz*." *Toni Morrison's Fiction: Contemporary Criticism.* Ed. David L. Middleton. *Critical Studies in Black Life and Culture.* New York: Garland, 2000. 297–309.

Middleton, David, ed. *Toni Morrison's Fiction: Contemporary Criticism. Critical Studies in Black Life and Culture.* New York: Garland, 2000.

Middleton, Joyce Irene. "Orality, Literacy, and Memory in Toni Morrison's *Song of Solomon*," *College English* 55.1 (Jan 1993): 64–75.

Morrison, Toni. *Lecture and Speech of Acceptance, upon the Award of the Nobel Prize for Literature, Delivered in Stockholm on the Seventh of December, Nineteen Hundred and Ninety-Three.* New York: Alfred A. Knopf, 1994.

———. *"The Dancing Mind": Speech upon Acceptance of the National Book Foundation Medal for Distinguished Contribution to American Letters on the Sixth of November Nineteen Hundred and Ninety-Six.* New York: Alfred A. Knopf, 1996.

———, ed. *Sightings and Rescue Missons: Fiction, Essays, and Conversations: Toni Cade Bambara.* New York: Pantheon, 1996.

———, ed. *Birth of a Nation'Hood: Gaze, Script, and Spectacle in the O.J. Simpson Case.* New York: Pantheon Books, 1997.

Nigro, Marie. "In Search of Self: Frustration and Denial in Toni Morrison's *Sula*." *Journal of Black Studies* 28.6 (Jul 1998): 724–737.

Novak, Phillip, "'Circles and Circles of Sorrow': In the wake of Morrison's *Sula*," *PMLA. Publications of the Modern Language Association of America* 114.2 (Mar 1999): 184–193.

Nowlin, Michael. "Toni Morrison's *Jazz* and the Racial Dreams of the American Writer," *American Literature* 71.1 (Mar 1999): 151–174.

Otten, Terry. *The Crime of Innocence in the Fiction of Toni Morrison.* Columbia: University of Missouri Press, 1991.

Pereira, Malin Walther. "Periodizing Toni Morrison's Work from *The Bluest Eye* to *Jazz*: The Importance of *Tar Baby*," *MELUS* 22.3 (Fall 1997): 71–82.

Phelan, James, "Sethe's Choice: *Beloved* and the Ethics of Reading" *Style* 32.2 (Summer 1998): 318–333.

Rigney, Barbara. *The Voices of Toni Morrison*. Ohio State University Press, 1991.

Ruas, Charles. *Conversations with American Writers*. New York: McGraw Hill, 1984.

Rubenstein, Roberta. "Singing the Blues/Reclaiming Jazz: Toni Morrison and Cultural Mourning," *Mosaic: A Journal for the Interdisciplinary Study of Literature* 31.2 (Jun 1998): 147–163.

Showalter, Elaine, ed. *Modern American Women Writers*. New York: Scribner, 1991.

Smith, Jessie Carney, ed. *Epic Lives: One Hundred Black Women Who Made a Difference*. Detroit: Visible Ink, 1993.

Smith, Valerie. *African-American Writers*. New York: Scribner, 1991.

Storhoff, Gary. "'Anaconda love': Parental enmeshment in Toni Morrison's *Song of Solomon*," *Style* 31.2 (Summer 1997): 290–309.

Tate, Claudia. *Black Women Writers*. New York: Continuum, 1983.

Taylor-Guthrie, Danille, ed. *Conversations with Toni Morrison*. Jackson: University Press of Mississippi, 1994.

Wilentz, Gay. "Civilizations Underneath: African Heritage as Cultural Discourse in Toni Morrison's *Song of Solomon*." *African-American Review* 26.1 (Spring 1992): 61–76.

Williams, Lisa. *The Artist as Outsider in the Novels of Toni Morrison & Virginia Woolf. Contributions in Women's Studies* Vol. 181. Greenwood, 2000.

Websites

Anniina's Toni Morrison Page
http://www.luminarium.org/contemporary/tonimorrison/

EducETH: Morrison, Toni
http://www.educeth.ch/english/readinglist/morrisont/

Online NewsHour: Toni Morrison—March 9, 1998
http://www.pbs.org/newshour/bb/entertainment/jan-june98/morrison_3-9.html

The Salon Interview: Toni Morrison
http://www.salon.com/books/int/1998/02/cov_si_02int.html

Toni Morrison, Winner of the 1993 Nobel Prize in Literature
http://nobelprizes.com/nobel/literature/1993a.html

The Toni Morrison Society
http://www.gsu.edu/~wwwtms/

Contributors

HAROLD BLOOM is Sterling Professor of the Humanities at Yale University and Henry W. and Albert A. Berg Professor of English at the New York University Graduate School. He is the author of over 20 books, including *Shelly's Mythmaking* (1959), *The Visionary Company* (1961), *Blake's Apocalypse* (1963), *Yeats* (1970), *A Map of Misreading* (1975), *Kabbalah and Criticism* (1975), *Agon: Toward a Theory of Revisionism* (1982), *The American Religion* (1992), *The Western Canon* (1994), and *Omens of Millennium: The Gnosis of Angels, Dreams, and Resurrection* (1996). *The Anxiety of Influence* (1973) sets forth Professor Bloom's provocative theory of the literary relationships between the great writers and their predecessors. His most recent books include *Shakespeare: The Invention of the Human*, a 1998 National Book Award finalist, and *How to Read and Why*, which was published in 2000. In 1999, Professor Bloom received the prestigious American Academy of Arts and Letters Gold Medal for Criticism.

ELLYN SANNA has authored more than 50 books, including adult nonfiction, novels, young adult biographies, and gift books. She also works as a freelance editor and manages Scriveners' Ink, an editorial service.

THOMAS MARCH received master's and doctoral degrees in English and American Literature from New York University. His primary research interest is 20th-century British and American literature, with special emphasis on the novel, psychoanalytic theory, and the representation of consciousness. He has published numerous essays on the work of 20th-century British and American writers, including George Orwell, E.M. Forster, Virginia Woolf, Anais Nin, Edmund Wilson, Saki, and Bessie Head. His short fiction and poetry have appeared in *Anais, Atenea, Verbatim*, and *The Yalobusha Review*. He is the co-author of *Assimilating New Leaders: The Key to Executive Retention*. In addition to completing the editing of his first monograph, *The Sympathetic Narrator*, Dr. March is currently editing a volume of essays on the representation of consciousness in literature.

CARL D. MALMGREN holds the position of Research Professor at the University of New Orleans. He is the author of *Fictional Space in the Modernist and Postmodernist American Novel* and *Worlds Apart: Narratology of Science Fiction*.

BARBARA CHRISTIAN has published numerous articles on race, gender, and literature. Her essay "Layered Rhythms: Virginia Woolf and Toni Morrison" appeared in the Fall/Winter 1993 issue of *Modern Fiction Studies*. She is also the author of *Black Women Novelists: The Development of a Tradition, 1892–1976*.

Index

Adventures of Huckleberry Finn, The, (Twain), 29
Atwood, Margaret
   on the slavery in *Beloved*, 68

Baby Suggs in *Beloved*
   his conversation with Paul D., 69–70
Bains, Guitar in *The Song of Solomon*
   challenges of friendship, 47–48, 51
Bayles, Martha
   blast of *Beloved*, 67
Beloved, 1, 18, 25, 33, 39
   based on Margaret Garner, 4–5
   consequences in, 55–56
   dedication of, 26
   dominant theme, 66–67
   as filling the gap of the African-American experience, 54–57
   generic identity in, 61–62
   as a ghost story, 61–66
   as historical, 65–66
   mixed genre and logic of slavery in, 61–73
   as a period piece, 1
   reincarnation in, 27
   release of, 3–4
   and *Sula*, 47
   supernatural dimension of, 67
   Sweet Home in, 55, 62
   as trilogy, 27

Beloved in *Beloved*
   ghost of dead daughter, 4, 25, 54, 63–65
   return to safe, 56
Benito Cereno, (Melville)
   inspiration to Morrison, 40
Birth of a Nation' Hood
   essays based on the O.J. Simpson Trials, 40
Black Book, The
   idea for *Beloved*, 25
   sharing the African-American history, 17
Blackburn, Sara
   on Morrison's dialogue, 15
Black Women Writers at Work
   quotes of Morrison, 16
Bloom, Harold
   introduction, 1–2
Bluest Eyes, The, 1, 4, 14, 17, 39, 41, 76–79
   accommodating nature in, 44
   assault on characters, 81
   the Bottom Community in, 80–82
   central theme, 80
   challenge of unnaturalness belief, 80
   community and nature in, 75, 85
   concern with hatred within, 43–44
   as Dick and Jane primer, 41
   language in, 86
   reviews of, 13

structural techniques in, 85
and *Sula*, 44–46
Bodwin, Mr. in *Beloved*
replacement for the School Teacher, 56
Boston Globe, The
interview with Morrison, 3–5
Breedlove, Mrs., in *The Bluest Eyes*
character analysis, 41–42
Breedlove, Pecola, in *The Bluest Eyes*, 13, 76, 85
character analysis, 42
feelings of unworthiness, 77
rape of, 80–81
and Shirley Temple, 43
Bryant, Jerry H.
critic of *Sula*, 16

Chicago Tribune, The
interview with Morrison, 10, 14
on *Jazz*, 27
Chicken Little in *Sula*
death as a defining moment, 46–47
Christian, Barbara
on community and nature in Morrison's novels, 75–91
on Morrison's character and belief system, 76
Claudia in *The Bluest Eyes*, 41, 47
introduction of, 85
Consolata in *Paradise*, 34, 58–59
Contemporary Literature
interview with Morrison, 37
Crouch, Stanley
on *Beloved* as exonerating Sethe, 67

Dalsgard, Katrine
community and culture in Morrison's work, 58
"Dancing Mind, The"
conditions that impede understanding, 59
Dead, Macon, in *The Song of Solomon*, 49, 51, 84

choices result in death, 84
goal of acquisition, 83
limits of African-American power, 48
obsession of, 48
representative of rising Northern Middle Class, 83
Dead, Milkman, in *The Song of Solomon*, 76, 79–80, 84, 90–91
challenges of friendship, 47–51
discovering the truth, 84
as hero, 2, 13
and Jadine in *Tar Baby*, 52
mercenary philosophy of, 89
his quest, 49
and Sula in *Sula*, 47–48
victory of, 51
Dead, Ruth in *The Song of Solomon*, 90–91
Deep Sightings and Rescue Missions, (Bambara)
preface by Morrison, 41
Denver in *Beloved*, 4
Dewall, James
on Morrison's characters, 52–53
Dorcas in *Jazz*, 27
murder of, 28, 57
relationship with Joe, 57
Dreaming Emmitt
award for, 24
characters in, 23–24
racism and slavery in, 22–23

Ella in *Beloved*
on love, 66
Encore American and World News
interview with Morrison, 14

Felice in *Jazz*
as a link to Dorca's memory, 57
Ford, Harold, 11–12, 29
Furman, Roger
work on *The Black Book*, 17
Friday in *Robinson Crusoe*, 29
and Clarence Thomas, 29

"Friday on the Potomac"
link to senate hearings, 29

Garner, Margaret
inspiration for *Beloved*, 4–5, 25
Gatehouse, Maggie in *Sula*, 44
Giddings, Paula
interview with Morrison, 14, 19

Hagar in *The Song of Solomon*, 84
Halle in *Beloved*, 69
Harris, Middleton A.
work on *The Black Book*, 17
Hill, Anita, 29

Jadine in *Tar Baby*
education of, 51–52
love with Son founded on escape, 53
and Milkman, 52
social prejudices, 52
Jazz, 1, 28, 33, 39
hope and tragedy in, 28
and *Tar Baby*, 56
theme of community misunderstandings, 56–57
as trilogy, 27

Knopf, Alfred A.
publisher of Morrison, 3–5

LeClair, Thomas
on *The Song of Solomon*, 19
on *Sula*, 16
Levitt, Morris
work on *The Black Book*, 17
Light in August, (Faulkner)
and *The Song of Solomon*, 2

Malmgren, Carl D.
on genre resistance, 63

the mixed genres and logic of slavery in *Beloved*, 61–73
'possession' in *Beloved*, 68
March, Thomas
on *Beloved*, 54–56
on *The Bluest Eyes*, 40–43
the fictional world of Morrison, 39–60
on *Jazz*, 56–57
on *Paradise*, 57–60
on race transcendence, 40
on *The Song of Solomon*, 47–51
on *Sula*, 44–51
on *Tar Baby*, 51–54
Margaret in *Tar Baby*
mental illness of, 51
Morgan, Decon in *Paradise*, 34, 58–59
Morgan, Steward in *Paradise*, 34, 58–59
Morrison, Harold, 11–12
Morrison, Slade, 29
Morrison, Toni
on African-American tradition, 17
and *Beloved*, 25–27, 61–74
biography of, 3–38
birth name, 5
and *The Black Book*, 17
on Black writers, 28–29
character belief system, 76
character's self-realization, 41–42
chronology, 93–94
on conservatism as fulfillment, 83
family life, 11–12
fictional world of, 39–60
individuality and community, 59–60
and 'manness', 44–45
nature and community in novels, 75–91
new challenges of, 17–21
the Nobel Prize for Literature, 30–33
novels of, 75–92
passion in writing, 12–14
race transcendence, 40
research of slavery, 24
response to criticism, 16

and the spiritual world, 7
on *Sula*, 44–46
teaching of, 18
tour for *Tar Baby*, 21–22
and the Writers Group, 11
works about, 97–100
works by, 95–96
Moses, Gilbert
director of *Dreaming Emmitt*, 23

Nation, The
on *Sula*, 16
Native Son, (Wright)
and *The Song of Solomon*, 20
New Leader, The
on *Beloved*, 26
New Republic, The
on *The Song of Solomon*, 19
on *Sula*, 16
Newsweek Magazine
interview with Morrison, 19
New York Times, The
on *Beloved*, 27
interview with Morrison, 7, 14
on Morrison's dialogue, 15
New York Times Best Seller List, The
placement of *Tar Baby*, 21
New York Times Book Review, The 12–14
and *The Song of Solomon*, 20
Nobel Prize for Literature, 1993
awarded to Morrison, 30–33
Novak, Phillip
observing *Beloved and Sula*, 47

Odine in *Tar Baby*, 51

Paradise, 1, 39
convent in, 57–58
destructive nature in, 57
story of, 33–37
and *Sula*, 57–58
as trilogy, 33

Parker, Betty Jean
interview with Morrison, 17
Paul D. in *Beloved*, 65, 69–70
condemning Sethe, 71
last of Sweet Home men, 62
on 'loving small', 66
representation of, 55
and Sethe, 55–56, 71–72
Pauline in *The Bluest Eyes*
loss of, 77
Peace, Eva in *Sula*, 46
bequeathed to daughters, 44–45
Peace, Sula in *Sula*, 14–16, 76
death, 46
defiance as defeat, 47, 82
and Milkman in *the Song of Solomon*, 47–49
and Nel in *Sula*, 44–47
rejection felt, 46
Pilate in *The Song of Solomon*, 48, 51, 84, 90
representation of nature, 83
Playing in the Dark: Whiteness and the Literary Imagination
as Morrison's project, 59–60
racial attitudes of early American authors, 28–29
Pulitzer Prize for Fiction, 1998
for *Beloved*, 5, 27

Race-Ing Justice, En–Gendering Power
response to controversy, 29
Random House, 12, 16, 18
Reba in *The Song of Solomon*, 84
Robinson Crusoe, (Defoe), 29

Sanna, Ellyn
biography of Morrison, 3–38
on *Beloved*, 25–27
on Morrison's Nobel Prize, 30–33
nature of evil in Morrison, 14–17
new challenges of Morrison, 17–21
Schoolteacher in *Beloved*, 55–56
Sethe in *Beloved*, 5, 65

and Beloved's appearance, 64
and Beloved's murder, 54, 67
ego formation, 69
keeping in the past, 62
naturalistic explanation, 64
and Paul D., 55–56, 71–72
reclaiming life, 56
repressed memory, 54
and slavery as a cause for actions, 70–71
Shapiro, Harold, 30
Sixo in *Beloved*, 69
  love for the Thirty-Mile Woman, 71
Smith, Ernest
  work on *The Black Book*, 17
Smith, Mrs. in *The Song of Solomon*
  suicide as sacrifice, 51
Son in *Tar Baby*, 52
  love with Jadine founded on escape, 53
Song of Solomon, The, 1, 20, 39, 76, 83
  community and nature in, 75, 85
  conflict with preoccupation of Earthly matters, 80–90
  contrast of values in, 84
  dedication of, 19
  element and structural point of reference, 88–89
  flight and abandonment in, 19
  forces that cement and challenge friendship, 47–48
  human capacity for misunderstanding, 51
  land dwellings, 80
  and *Light in August*, 2
  and *Native Son*, 20
  past myth merging with the present, 91
  as permanent work, 2
  recognition of, 20–21
  sales of, 35
  story of, 18–19
  and *Tar Baby*, 53–54
  two Black Communities in, 79–80
Southern Review, The
  on *Beloved*, 26

Street, Valerie in *Tar Baby*
  on ignoring the signs, 51
Sturdy Black Bridges
  interview with Morrison, 17
Sula, 1, 17–18, 39, 76
  award, 15
  and *The Bluest Eyes*, 44, 46
  the Bottom's beginning in, 77–79, 82–83
  community and nature in, 75, 85
  controversy in, 16
  death in, 83
  dedication of, 15
  image of fire and water in, 87–88
  individuality and defiance in, 44–46
  insularity of land, 78
  'manness' in, 44–45, 83
  primal elements, 86
  prologue and epilogue, 86–87
  story of, 14–16, 44–51
  struggle, 88
  and *Tar Baby*, 56
Sydney in *Tar Baby*, 51

Tar Baby, 23, 39
  based on childhood story of Uncle Remus, 21
  as direct assault, 51
  and *Jazz*, 57
  reviews of, 21–22
  and *The Song of Solomon*, 53–54
Tate, Claudia
  quoting Morrison, 16
Thirty-Mile Woman in *Beloved*, 71
Thomas, Clarence, 29
Till, Emmitt in *Dreaming Emmitt*, 23–24
Time Magazine
  interview with Morrison, 31–32, 34, 36–37
Trace, Joe in *Jazz*, 27, 56–57
  on Killing Dorcas, 28
  relationship with Dorcas, 57
  struggle of, 57

Valerian in *Tar Baby*, 52
Violet in *Jazz*, 27, 56–57
  struggle of, 57

Watkins, Mel
  interview with Morrison, 21
Winfrey, Oprah
  purchasing the screenplay of *Beloved*, 35–6
  as Sethe in film *Beloved*, 5
Wofford, George and Ramah
  parents of Morrison, 5–8
Wright Jude in *Sula*, 46
Wright, Nel in *Sula*, 14–16, 78, 82
  and Milkman in *The Song of Solomon*, 49
  and Sula, 44–47